EARLY CHILDHOOD EDUCATION
Leslie R. Williams, Editor

What If All the Kids Are White?

Anti-Bias Multicultural Education with Young Children and Families

LOUISE DERMAN-SPARKS
PATRICIA G. RAMSEY
with Julie Olsen Edwards

Foreword by Carol Brunson Day

Teachers College, Columbia University
New York and London

The poem in Chapter 6 entitled "Diversity: Noun, Adjective, or Verb?" is reprinted by permission of its author, Katie Kissinger.

Appendix D: "What Do Trees Have to Do with Peace?" by Denise Roy is reprinted from the FamilySpirit Newsletter: Winter 2004 (www.familyspirit.com). Copyright © 2004 by Denise Roy. Reprinted by permission of the author.

Published by Teachers College Press, 1234 Amsterdam Avenue, New York, NY 10027

Library of Congress Cataloging-in-Publication Data

Derman Sparks, Louise.
    What if all the kids are white? : anti-bias multicultural education with young children and families / Louise Derman-Sparks, Patricia G. Ramsey, with Julie Olsen Edwards ; foreword by Carol Brunson Day.
       p.   cm. — (Early childhood education series)
    Includes bibliographical references (p.   ) and index.
    ISBN-13: 978-0-8077-4678-3 (cloth : alk. paper)
    ISBN-l0: 0-8077-4678-9 (cloth : alk. paper)
    ISBN-13: 978-0-8077-4677-6 (pbk. : alk. paper)
    ISBN-l0: 0-8077-4677-0 (pbk : alk. paper)
    1. Multicultural education—United States.   2. Racism—Study and teaching (Early childhood)—United States.   3. Whites—Race identity—United States.   I. Ramsey, Patricia G.   II. Edwards, Julie Olsen. III. Title.   IV. Series.
    LC1099.3.D47 2006
    370.117—dc22   2005056865

ISBN-13:   ISBN-10:
978-0-8077-4677-6 (paper)   0-8077-4677-0 (paper)
978-0-8077-4678-3 (cloth)   0-8077-4678-9 (cloth)

Printed on acid-free paper
Manufactured in the United States of America

13   12   11   10   09   08   07   06   8   7   6   5   4   3   2

FROM LOUISE:
To Dorothy Healey,
who taught me that analysis and practice
must always be partners

FROM PATTY:
To Leslie Williams,
beloved friend, wise mentor,
and fun-loving adventurer

Contents

Foreword

What do you do when you want to attract a broad audience of readers interested in anti-bias and multicultural education and at the same time pique the interest of whites to examine themselves? Louise Derman-Sparks and Patricia Ramsey's bold and provocative title is no doubt one good way if it creates for you, as it did for me, a cognitive imbalance that gets curiosity and emotion churning. For, to the extent that our approach to the study of racism only admonishes whites to change their behavior toward its victims, it also directs curiosity and emotion away from whites examining their own whiteness.

But this examination is a necessary one, growing out of what we have discovered about the complexities of how racism perpetuates itself. These writers' conviction that we *can* be comfortable with whites "retreating into" their whiteness and focusing on a deeper understanding of it is a step that can bring us closer to our ultimate goal. For Derman-Sparks and Ramsey offer an "alternative vision" for white identity that breaks the mold and refuses to accept the unspoken assumptions for whites being white. Their challenge is for whites to become critical thinkers about the history that they learned in school and that they continue to relearn. They examine the most difficult of topics—and explore the long-overdue treatment of whites NOT as homogeneous, but as a group with intricate variety, unraveling privilege and social class differences in depth, acknowledging that the material advantages of being white are not equally distributed.

In the process they provide plenty of concrete suggestions and ideas to engage and struggle with. Yet, their expert message comes with plenty of assurance that this is no recipe book. Rather the participants in the process will construct the solutions for change.

Derman-Sparks and Ramsey's personal histories and professional trajectories demanded that they write this book. And the current status of our anti-bias work demands we read it and use it well.

Are whites really ready to learn how to have the conversation about racism among themselves? Though I am not white, I feel strongly that it is time. And I believe that the presence of this book in your hands represents a marker for a maturity point in the anti-bias multicultural movement in early childhood education. I feel thankful to have an approach with such integrity—integrity made possible by the work that has been accomplished in early childhood education so far, work that has as it highest goal solidarity among activists of all backgrounds who want to build a just and sustainable society with equitable distribution of resources.

—Carol Brunson Day, Ph.D.

Acknowledgments

Writing this book has been a collaborative project from start to finish. Not only have we (Patty and Louise) worked together on every aspect of it, but many friends and colleagues have joined us along the way.

First we would like to thank our home institutions for the time and financial support for this project. We started this project while Patty was on sabbatical from Mount Holyoke College, which also provided a small grant for Jane Schall, who gathered anecdotal material from teachers and creatively helped us solve some of the tricky organizational and writing challenges. Louise was able to include writing as part of her workload at Pacific Oaks College. Special thanks to her colleagues and Corrine McGuigan, Provost, who understood when the book had to take precedence over other work.

Second, we feel deep gratitude to the many people who read the manuscript at various stages and gave us supportive yet honest critical feedback and provided us with compelling stories and examples. They include (in alphabetical order) Lynne Brill, Catherine Goins, Janet Gonsolez-Mena, Eric Hoffman, Suzanne Jones, Mary Pat Martin, Debbie Revaçon, Marilyn Segal, and Meg Thomas. In addition, a special word of appreciation to Julie Olsen Edwards, whose insightful assistance was invaluable in revising the first completed version of our manuscript.

We also pay homage to the many friends, colleagues, and sister/fellow anti-racism activists who have inspired, informed, and supported our work over the decades. They include: Joe Barndt, Babette Brown, Brad Chambers, Ron Chisom, Fran Davison, Carol Brunson Day, Catherine Goins, Sandra Lawrence, Mary Pat Martin, Deborah Menkart, Sonia Nieto, Anne Stewart, Beverly Daniel Tatum, Nahdiyah Faquir Taylor, Ellen Wolpert, Sheli Wortis, and Louise's many Crossroads' Ministry and Pacific Oaks Colleagues.

We also acknowledge the many teachers throughout the country who have taught us what Anti-Bias/Multicultural work means in practice. A special thanks to the wonderful teachers at Gorse Child Study Center at Mount Holyoke: Barbara Sweeney, Janna Aldrich, Valerie Sawka, Carole

Lynche, Sandy Johnson, and Sukey Heard, whose wisdom and stories are woven into many of our examples. Another special thanks to the teachers in Australia who shared their experiences with us.

Susan Liddicoat, acquisitions editor at Teachers College Press, has been our friend and editor for many years. Both of us, on separate projects, have benefited enormously from her honest yet supportive feedback, her creativity, and her commitment to bring out the best in our ideas and writing. From the very first time we mentioned this book to her, Susan was excited and encouraging and pushed us to keep on writing and re-working the book until it was where we all wanted it to be. Sadly, this book may be one of the last that she will work on as a full-time editor because she retired in September 2005. We and many other TC Press authors will miss her support and willingness to push for projects that she feels are worthwhile. Most of all we will miss her formidable editing skills and our enlightening conversations. . . .

Finally, of course, we thank our families for their support and willingness to plan their lives around our work. I (Patty) thank my sons, Daniel and Tuto, whose adolescent struggles have made me realize the urgency of this work, the need to create a more caring and hospitable world for all children—one that does not require that children choose who they are based on racial and ethnic categories that divide us from one another. To Fred Moseley, my wonderful partner and co-parent, thank you for your unflagging support and caring as we ride the roller coaster of raising adolescents together! I (Louise) thank my son and daughter, Douglass and Holly, for all their love and encouragement. In the end, it is for them that I do this work. My eternal gratitude to Bill, my partner in life and in anti-bias education work, for understanding from the beginning what I was doing and why.

What If All the Kids Are White?

Anti-Bias Multicultural Education
with Young Children and Families

Why a Book About White Children?

> All the kids in my program are white. Not only that, but most of them are blond and come from similar ethnic and economic backgrounds. I want to use an anti-bias curriculum, but how can I bring up diversity to this group in a meaningful way?
> —Comments and question raised during an anti-bias workshop

"What if all the kids are white?" has been one of the most frequently asked questions in our workshops and discussions with early childhood teachers over the past 2 decades. Almost always posed by white teachers, it echoes the persistent confusion about the role of whites in the multicultural movement and, in particular, the engagement of white children, families, and teachers in multicultural education.

Over the years, the question has remained the same, but its tone and meaning have changed. In the early days of multicultural education, teachers in predominately white programs often assumed that multicultural education was not relevant to their children, and the question had an undertone of, Why should we bother? After all, *their* children were not confronted by negative, identity-damaging stereotypes and alienated from images and practices in their classrooms. More recently, however, many teachers of white children have become aware of how discrimination affects everyone. They understand that a false sense of racial superiority is damaging, causes isolation, and ill prepares children to function in a diverse society. Such teachers also recognize that working for social justice will benefit *all* people, but cannot be achieved unless people in all groups, including whites, join the long-term struggle. Thus, many teachers today believe that anti-bias/multicultural education *is* relevant to white children but do not know how to engage children in learning about differences and social justice in the absence of obvious diversity and disadvantages to

1

"work with." As a result, the intent of the question has shifted from why to how.

In addition, many activists and theorists engaged in the movement for social justice here and abroad have become increasingly interested in identifying the specific dynamics of "whiteness" and the role of whites in challenging racism. They argue that racism must be understood as a systemic, institutionalized force that advantages people defined as "white" and disadvantages people defined as "not white." Understanding that racism is not just a matter of individual prejudice and discrimination opens up new avenues for defining the roles and responsibilities of whites. We now understand that it is not enough for white people to "accept" and "respect" people of color or to "tweak" the current system. Rather, whites need to undergo a profound shift from viewing the world through a lens of dominance, however unrecognized, to making a commitment to equitably sharing power and resources.

AN ALTERNATIVE VISION OF WHITE IDENTITY

Whites often fear that they will have much to lose if racism ends, but in fact they have much to gain. Racism exacts a cost from both those who are hurt and those who benefit from it; the ending of racism will be both humanizing and liberating to all. Thirty-five years ago, Robert Terry (1970) proposed the following image of a "new white consciousness":

> The *new* in the label points to fresh possibilities. We are not totally limited by our past. *White* is a constant reminder that we are not racially neutral, and also a reminder that we still participate in racist institutions and culture. *Consciousness* continually reminds us that we need to reconstruct totally our understanding of who we are and what we ought to do. (p. 20)

Terry ended his book with a hopeful and motivating call to whites:

> *"The new white committed to justice and working to rid this nation of its racism can be a major force for social justice.* The time is right. *It is up to us to seize that time to turn our legacy of old white privilege into new white possibility."* (p. 97; emphasis in original)

At the time, this work received little notice, but now these ideas have gained momentum. Since the late 1990s many authors (e.g., Bardnt, 1991; C. S. Brown, 2002; Howard, 1999; Kincheloe, Steinberg, Rodriguez, & Chennault,

1998; Kivel, 2002; Rothenberg, 2002) have focused on how whites perpetuate racism and how they may be engaged in anti-bias work.

This paradigm shift calls on educators and families to nurture white
children's early identity and social-emotional development in new ways.
It is not enough to teach them to embrace racial and cultural diversity;
children must also develop individual and group identities that will recognize and resist the false notions of racial superiority and racial entitlement. To participate in this work, those of us who are white must also
develop our own new white consciousness.

In this book, we are highlighting one aspect of anti-bias/multicultural
education work, much as a map insert magnifies one piece of the overall
terrain. *What If All the Kids Are White?* is not a substitute for books that
discuss the multiple aspects of anti-bias/multicultural curriculum (e.g.,
Derman-Sparks & ABC Task Force, 1989; Ramsey, 2004). Rather, it is written for readers who are familiar with anti-bias/multicultural work but
wish to explore the theoretical and practical ramifications of whiteness
in more depth.

The focus on white children in no way implies that their needs and
interests should be the "front and center" of anti-bias/multicultural education. We write this book, not to detract from programs and curricula that
support children and families of color, but rather to increase the possibilities that white children will grow up to join them in the ongoing struggles
for social justice. As Lewis (2001) says, "We must ask ourselves, can much
change if the educational experiences of White middle-class children do
not undergo some transformations?" (p. 805).

As you may have noticed, we are using the term *anti-bias/multicultural*
to describe our work. Multicultural education, which had its roots in the
racial inequities that fueled the civil rights movement, has gone through
many phases since its inception in the 1970s. It has broadened its scope and
has shifted from a focus on cultural pluralism to critical thinking (see P. G.
Ramsey & Williams, 2003, for a more detailed discussion of this history).
In the early childhood field, the publication of *Anti-Bias Curriculum: Tools
for Empowering Young Children* in 1989 (Derman-Sparks & A.B.C. Task
Force) was pivotal in shifting the focus of early childhood multicultural
education from "appreciating diversity" to working toward social justice.
In this current book we use the term *anti-bias/multicultural education* to
embrace this 30-year history and to emphasize the struggle toward social,
economic, and cultural equity.

Since both of us live and work in the United States, this book focuses
primarily on the dynamics of racism and anti-racism work in the United
States. However, writers and teachers in other countries, in particular

Australia and Britain, have also discussed and addressed these issues. While there are historical and political differences between countries, many power and personal dynamics are similar. Therefore, we have used some examples from different countries and hope that readers in other parts of the world may find this book helpful and be able to adapt the suggestions to fit their particular issues and circumstances.

We wrote this book for all teachers, caregivers, and family members who work with or raise white children. The conceptual framework and learning themes are relevant for white children and families in either homogeneous or racially/ethnically diverse settings, although specific approaches and activities vary across programs. We hope that white teachers will gain new and deeper insights into their identities, ideas, and practices and that teachers of color will add to their knowledge about the dynamics of whiteness. Our ultimate aim is to open up new conversations that enhance the likelihood that white children will grow up to resist and challenge racism in its many forms.

CORE LEARNING THEMES

We propose seven core learning themes for working with white children. They are derived from the four anti-bias education goals, listed in Figure I.1. (Derman-Sparks et al., 1989) and reflect our understanding of the construction of "whiteness" in our society.

1. Develop authentic identities based on personal abilities and interests, family history, and culture, rather than on white superiority. (ABC Goal 1)
2. Know, respect, and value the range of the diversity of physical and social attributes among white people. (ABC Goal 1)
3. Build the capacity for caring, cooperative, and equitable relationships with others. (ABC Goal 2)
4. Understand, appreciate, and respect differences and similarities beyond the immediate family, neighborhood center/classroom, and racial group. (ABC Goal 2)
5. Learn to identify and challenge stereotypes, prejudice, and discriminatory practices among themselves and in the immediate environment. (ABC Goals 2 and 3)
6. Commit to the ideal that all people have the right to a secure, healthy, comfortable, and sustainable life and that everyone must equitably share the resources of the earth and collaboratively care for them. (ABC Goals 3 and 4)

Figure I.1: Anti-Bias Education Goals
Louise Derman-Sparks

The underlying intent of anti-bias education is to foster the development of children and adults who have the personal strength, critical-thinking ability, and activist skills to work with others to build caring, just, diverse communities and societies for all.

Goal 1: **Nurture each child's construction of a knowledgeable, confident self-concept and group identity.**
This goal means creating the educational conditions in which all children are able to like who they are without needing to feel superior to anyone else. It also means enabling children to develop biculturally—to be able to effectively interact within their home culture and within the dominant culture.

Goal 2: **Promote each child's comfortable, empathic interaction with people from diverse backgrounds.**
This goal means guiding children's development of the cognitive awareness, emotional disposition, and behavioral skills needed to respectfully and effectively learn about differences, comfortably negotiate and adapt to differences, and cognitively understand and emotionally accept the common humanity that all people share.

Goal 3: **Foster each child's critical thinking about bias.**
This goal means guiding children's development of the cognitive skills to identify "unfair" and "untrue" images (stereotypes), comments (teasing, name-calling) and behaviors (discrimination) directed at one's own or others' identities (be they gender, race, ethnicity, disability, class, age, or weight) *and* having the emotional empathy to know that bias hurts.

Goal 4: **Cultivate each child's ability to stand up for her/himself and for others in the face of bias.**
This "activism" goal includes helping every child learn and practice a variety of ways to act when another child acts in a biased manner toward her/him, when a child acts in a biased manner toward another child, or when an adult acts in a biased manner. Goal 4 builds on Goal 3: Critical thinking and empathy are necessary components of acting for oneself or others in the face of bias.

Note: The four goals are for *all* children: They interact with and build on one another. The specific tasks and strategies for working toward these goals will depend on children's backgrounds, ages, and life experiences.

7. Build identities that include anti-bias ideals and possibilities and acquire skills and confidence to work together for social justice in their own classrooms and communities and in the larger society. (ABC Goal 4)

BOOK ORGANIZATION

Chapter 1 continues the introduction to the issues that this book explores, this time from the perspective of early childhood educators. The rest of the book is divided into two parts. Part I (Chapters 2, 3, 4, and 5) focuses on the construction of whiteness and white identity. Part II (Chapters 6, 7, 8, and 9) focuses on expanding and deepening the sense of connection among the human family and the capacity for critical thinking and activism. Both parts have a parallel construction: first, a chapter describing the historical roots of the main themes of that part; second, a chapter reviewing relevant research on children's development; third, a chapter illustrating how this information can be applied to working with children; fourth, a chapter on ways to engage adults in these issues. To enhance your interaction with the book content, we have added reflection questions to several chapters as well as suggestions for further reading. At the end of both Part I and Part II, we conclude with "A Tale of Two Centers": Each episode illustrates how specific learning themes might be implemented in two different early childhood programs. (If stories help you understand conceptual issues, then you may want to peek at these first. However, you will better understand them after reading through the previous chapters.)

Appendix A includes a list of children's books and curriculum resources to support classroom activities. To help readers begin to learn more about anti-racist movements in the United States, we have included Appendix B, a list of organizations and websites, and Appendix C, a chart of 20th-century white anti-racist activists. Appendix D is an article about Wangari Maathai, winner of the 2004 Nobel Peace Prize, entitled "What Do Trees Have to Do with Peace?"

In your eagerness to learn how to implement the ideas in this book, you may be tempted to skip the history and research chapters (2, 3, 6, 7). We *strongly* urge you to resist doing that. Anti-bias/multicultural teaching is not a matter of simply carrying out a collection of activities. It is a complex of large and small decisions that reflect our life histories, beliefs, and knowledge about children and the contexts of their lives. Often the best curriculum arises from a spontaneous event such as a child's question, a community event, or a family's concern. Generating curriculum that is responsive to current issues and appropriate for a particular group of children requires a deep understanding of how the learning themes and children's development reflect the larger social-political dynamics.

Thus, it is crucial to take the time to reflect about the broad social and economic context, your specific community, your own life, and the families with whom you work. In particular, knowledge about the history of the social-political construct of "whiteness" makes clear that absorbing the power codes of racism is not the "fault" of individual children or families, but an inevitable outcome of growing up in a racist society. Conversely, an appreciation of the history of white anti-racism activism can inspire teachers, children, and families to push past their fears and practical concerns and join with people who are working for a society where the right to the pursuit of life, liberty, and happiness is truly shared by all people.

OUR OWN BACKGROUNDS

At this point, we believe it is important to tell you a little about ourselves, since all authors' life experiences deeply influence their thinking and writing. We first connected 20 years ago, when both of us were in the early stage of developing our work about the harm racism and other "isms" inflict on young children and the implications for early childhood education practice. We met at an NAEYC annual conference in Denver, talked for many hours in a quiet restaurant off the beaten track, and became lifelong colleagues and friends. We have learned from, supported, and collaborated with each other since that meeting. As two white women, we continually work to come to terms with our roles as anti-bias, anti-racist, multicultural educators in a white-dominated society. Like many, we balance and struggle between our dual realities of working to eliminate the racial inequities of our society and recognizing that personally we benefit from them as long as they exist. We believe that while it is not possible to undo history, it *is* possible to learn from it and to create a new future.

Louise

I have been a teacher for 40 years, first of preschool children and then of adults. I grew up in a white, Jewish American, working-class, activist family in Brooklyn and Manhattan, New York. My parents told me that I began asking, "Why?" almost as soon as I could talk, soon followed by, "It isn't fair!" I was very lucky to have parents who believed in working for social change. I learned about activism from an early age, by observing and listening and by accompanying my parents on some of their community activism work.

I went to public schools, from kindergarten through college. In elementary and junior high school, a few very good teachers illuminated the possibilities of caring and meaningful education. I was fortunate to attend the High School of Music and Art, which we would now call a public "magnet" school. In a high school more diverse than most in New York City at that time, I found my voice and began becoming an activist in my own right.

Over the many years of doing social justice and anti-bias work, I have had to deepen my understanding of the multiple parts of my identity. My parents taught me that I had a responsibility to work with others to end racism, but our whiteness was only an indirect reality—never overtly mentioned. But then came the growing Black Power/Black Liberation movement, raising profound and disturbing questions about the roles and behaviors of whites in the civil rights movement. These concerns were clarified for me by Robert Terry's book *For Whites Only* (1970), which made clear an appropriate agenda for whites wanting to end racism.

Reconstructing the meaning of a white identity also required rethinking other facets of who I was. For one it raised new questions about what it means to be Jewish. The lightning flashed when, in the mid-1970s, I read Albert Memmi's *The Colonizer and the Colonized* (1965), which argued that Jewish people have a foot in both worlds—in his language, that of the oppressor and that of the oppressed. Putting this concept into the U.S. context, I came to understand that whiteness enabled Jewish people to gain benefits from systemic racism *and* that these privileges could be withdrawn at any time, making Jewish people the targets of oppression.

In addition, I continue to figure out how my class and gender identity fit together with my white identity. While the anti-racism movement challenged me to examine my role on the *advantaged* side of societal power, the women's movement gave me the language and analysis to understand sexism, which put me on the *disadvantaged* side. Within my family of origin and as an early childhood teacher, I am working class. Now I am college professor, of a different socioeconomic status, but I continue to identify with my working-class roots. I am also the mother of two grown, adopted children, who each has a white birth mother and an African American birth father. While this does not change my own racial privilege, I suffered the anger and pain of seeing my children experience racism in their lives.

So, I am white and, as said before, gain many privileges in this society. That's a simple reality. At the same time, the other facets of my identity make my reality more complex. Both the simplicity and the complexity of my reality are not unique to me. Rather, both must be considered as we try to figure out what it means to raise and teach white children to join in the building of a more just society and world.

Patty

Like Louise, I have benefited from the economic, educational, and political advantages of being white. However, I have additional layers of privilege and resistance to change and often wish that I had been raised in a politically activist family, as Louise was. My ancestors, representing different strands of Protestantism, came from England, Scotland, the Netherlands, and Germany. Many came to the United States during the 17th and early 18th centuries, well before the American Revolution. Although they were escaping poverty and, in some cases, religious and political persecution at home, they benefited from their status as white Anglo-Saxon Protestants once they arrived on these shores. Most of my ancestors were people of modest means—small farmers, shopkeepers, carpenters, teachers, and ministers—not wealthy, but also not victims of racist ideologies as were members of many groups (including Europeans, among them Italian, Irish, and Jewish immigrants). Moreover, across generations, my forebears benefited from the growing wealth in this country and became comfortably middle class.

My parents were good middle-class "liberals." They supported the civil rights movement and were horrified at the segregation in the South and the resistance to school desegregation in Boston. However, they were not activists, and these issues never intruded on our daily lives. We lived only a few miles away from the turbulent Boston schools, but in our virtually all-white suburb, busing was simply a way to get to school, not a source of riots and flying rocks.

Despite my privileged and, for the most part, unchallenged status, I also remember, from a very young age, feeling that something was wrong; that I was only seeing a thin slice of reality, always the crescent and never the full moon. When we drove through poor neighborhoods (with the doors locked, of course!), I was afraid. Yet I also sensed a vibrancy that was missing in my well-manicured suburb. As a good white, however, I kept my silence and did not rock the boat with questions. The first time I spoke up was in high school, when I came face to face with the effects of anti-Semitism. Not only had the administration dismissed my Jewish friends' discomfort about performing in a highly religious Christmas concert, but they also systematically excluded them from receiving certain awards. My first "political action" was going with a group to the school administration and trying to persuade them to change these discriminatory practices.

I also grew up believing that I had "no culture." I envied my Jewish and Italian friends, for their ethnic communities, vibrant holiday celebrations, traditional foods, and religious ceremonies. My life seemed very bland and ordinary in comparison. Looking back I realize that because my life fit the "invisible norms" of the white middle class, I could not see that, indeed, I was learning particular cultural values and ways of being in the world. Most important, my yearning for more ethnic connections often blinded me to the power and privilege that I unconsciously absorbed and enjoyed.

With many lurches and missteps, I have spent most of my adult life trying to broaden my perspective, to uncover and challenge my biases, and to resist injustice. Many experiences—working in Honduras, serving 2 years as a VISTA, (Volunteers in Service to America) volunteer in a Mexican American community in California, living in Mexico for 2 years as a parent of young children—have made me acutely aware of my cultural blinders and economic advantages and have forced me to examine my biases and assumptions. Most recently, parenting two teenagers who are both adopted from Chile has laid bare my white middle-class assumptions about schooling and academic "success." I have been immersed in the painful reality of the pressures and invalidation that children of color experience even with the most well intentioned and highly trained teachers.

Writing this book has forced me to revisit, reconsider, and rethink my own racial and anti-bias identity. It has prompted questions that have led to my learning about several ancestors who were abolitionists, enabling me to connect with my family's history in new ways. I participate in writing this book in the spirit of humility, knowing that I will never be completely free of assumptions and actions that reflect my unearned privilege as a white person. Nor will I ever fully understand the lived experience of those who have been penalized by the same system that has elevated my family. However, I also write with hope that this book will encourage readers to push through their fears and resistance, to examine their lives and assumptions more closely, and to consider how we might work together to change the way that white children learn about the world.

We invite you to join with us in this much needed conversation about how to "grow" white children who will strive for a society without racism and thrive in a just, equitable, peaceful, multicultural world.

CHAPTER 1

Ideals to Practice

I loved your multicultural workshop; I felt really inspired to come back to my center and work on these issues with the kids and families. But whenever I try something, it never goes the way that I had planned, and then I get anxious about saying or doing the wrong thing, and the whole thing falls kind of flat.

—E-mail message from a teacher who had attended a workshop a few months earlier

Teachers often express similar reactions when they begin to apply anti-bias/multicultural (AB/MC) concepts in their classroom and encounter their own anxieties or resistance from other. Yet many continue to build AB/MC curriculum and to surmount multiple obstacles. Why? What motivates teachers to persist in working with material that is so complex and emotionally charged?

Something happens. You hear a child refuse to play with another child because "he's too fat!" You see a group of children laughing at a new class member who speaks with an accent. Three little girls (all white) play in the costume corner, and one says, "I get to be princess 'cuz I've got blonde hair," and the other girls agree without comment. You hear a child refuse to play with the dark-skinned doll, because "it's dirty."

Something happens. And because you care about children, care about helping them live joyfully in a diverse world, can't bear to see children hurt or learning fear and bias, you feel that you have to do something. You know that if you wait until you are completely sure of yourself, the moment will pass. If you wait until you know enough, another generation of children will be in your care and the children you work with now will have more deeply learned prejudiced attitudes. (J. O. Edwards, personal communication, April 2005)

Doing AB/MC work with white children and families, especially on race and racism, is pioneering. The destination is a vision; we construct the paths to our destination as we walk them. Mistakes are inevitable. Like all deeply important curriculum, this work requires preparation, constant tending, enthusiasm, and commitment. It also requires faith in the outcome, as Eric Hoffman, an experienced anti-bias early childhood educator explains: "I try to provide experiences that will sow the seeds of change. Then, sooner or later, children will incorporate those experiences into their thinking. I've learned it takes concrete experience, time, and faith in their intelligence" (quoted in Alvarado, Derman-Sparks, & Ramsey, 1999, p. 89).

Sometimes teachers must overcome their own doubts: "As I've been doing this work, I've found that most of the resistance I've met has been my own—feeling uncomfortable, feeling I wasn't ready. . . . But I would go ahead, and for the most part, it would turn out fine. I'd be glad that I took the chance" (Barbara Yasui, quoted in Alvarado et al., 1999, p. 167). It also has the possibility of great rewards as teachers gain confidence in their work. Beth Wallace speaks for many when she affirms that "for me, anti-bias work is about wholeness. It allows me to . . . keep intact the fabric of my convictions about children, equity, and social justice" (quoted in Alvarado et al., 1999, p. 155).

Unfortunately, for most whites, neither their education nor their life experiences provide the knowledge, analysis, and critical thinking skills about racism and other "isms" to create a solid foundation for doing AB/MC work. They lack role models who openly and directly talk about race and racism (or other forms of diversity and inequalities) with adults or children. Indeed, most whites are raised with silence on these topics, with the tacit message that such conversations are neither appropriate nor polite. So when children make comments that require direct responses, teachers often panic and are unable to use the knowledge and skills they do have, as illustrated by the following account:

> Darcy was talking with her kindergarteners (90% white and 10% Asian American) about the many ways that people cook rice, which was part of a larger curriculum on food. Mei, Eileen's mother, a Chinese American woman, was in the classroom that day to do a cooking project with the children. As Darcy was showing the children photographs of families from many different countries cooking and eating rice, one white girl asked in a loud voice, "Why do Chinese people have funny eyes?" Darcy felt her mouth go dry and her stomach lurch. She glanced at Mei and saw

that Mei and Eileen were both looking down. She knew that she should say something, but wasn't sure what to say and was afraid of making things worse. So she took a deep breath and went back to the topic of rice and introduced the cooking activity that Mei was going to do. Afterward, talking to her supervisor, she realized how she often panicked when the subject of race and racial prejudice came up openly, especially if she was in the presence of people from different racial groups. She also worried that her discomfort had been obvious to the children and that in her rush to get to "safe ground" (i.e., the cooking project) she had probably reinforced the idea that Chinese people have "funny eyes."

Darcy and her supervisor brainstormed some ideas about what she could have done and talked about developing a curriculum about similarities and differences to use as a context for helping the children to appreciate the uniqueness of everyone's eyes and other facial features. The supervisor also decided to initiate a staff discussion group about the challenges of talking about race with young children.

Aside from growing up silenced about race, teachers are also stymied by insufficient professional training for doing AB/MC work. A few in-service workshops or an add-on module in a college class are not enough preparation to authentically raise and explore these issues with adults and children (Chang, Muckelroy, & Pulido-Tobiassen, 1996). But the children won't wait; teachers need to avoid becoming paralyzed and must risk acting, even before they feel totally ready. As Hoffman says,

> Anything I try will be unsatisfactory to someone, make someone uncomfortable, or cause a conflict. But if I try to meet every possible criticism before I take action, I will be paralyzed. So I've got to keep moving ahead with my best thinking, learn from the results, listen to the criticism, and try again. (quoted in Alvarado et al. 1999, p. 106)

Despite these obstacles, many teachers working with white children *do* find ways of engaging children and families in meaningful ways around issues of bias and racial identity. They diffuse resistance, they garner support, and they set out on their new path with courage and commitment.

Krista, an Anglo-Australian teacher who teaches kindergarten in an elite all-white school in Australia, found ways to overcome parental resistance and ease the children and families into an AB/MC curriculum as seen in the story that follows. (While the details reflect the history and people of Australia, the lessons also apply to programs here in the United States).

Active in a movement working toward gaining equal rights and resources for the Aboriginal People [who, like Native Americans, were stripped of their lands and ways of life by European colonizers], Krista wanted to include these issues in her kindergarten curriculum. However, when she mentioned her political work to the parents, she mostly got blank stares, and the subject would quickly change. In some cases, parents were overtly hostile, dismissing the Aboriginal People as "lazy" and "living off the dole." Thus, she knew that she would have to start in a slow, nonthreatening way.

Krista initially focused on learning about the families' backgrounds and invited parents to share their family stories in the classroom. Meanwhile, she slowly introduced some Aboriginal art and stories in the classroom. The children, unlike their parents, were very interested. She decided to build on the children's enthusiasm and began weaving stories, artwork, foods, and toys that reflected different Aboriginal groups into the curriculum. Often she pointed out similarities between the Aboriginal stories and the family stories that parents were sharing. Krista's Aboriginal friends from the movement often visited and told stories or did art projects with the children. Krista always invited parents to come when there was a guest, and as they heard their children's excited descriptions, more parents began to participate. A couple of guests came several times, and the parents and children got to know them personally.

Inevitably, some parents began to object to the emphasis on Aboriginal life in the curriculum. Krista proposed a meeting where they could air their concerns. By this time other parents had become enthusiastic, and they took the lead in defending the curriculum. In particular, they helped the resistant parents see how, as Australians, the children needed to know the full history of Australia, not simply the Anglo-Australian story that dominated the textbooks that children would be reading as they got older.

Krista also tape-recorded a number of the conversations she had with the children about these issues. One parent who had become very supportive of the curriculum transcribed the conversations (the parts that were most interesting) and put these transcripts into a loose-leaf notebook that was left on a table outside the classroom for parents to read and comment on. In this way parents could get firsthand accounts of how Krista and the guests were talking with the children and how the children were responding. As they read these transcripts, many parents began to remember the negative messages about Aboriginal People that they had learned as children and to recognize the limitations and biases in their views of Australia. They started to see how Krista's work was relevant to their own lives. A telling moment came when one of the transcripts reported a conversation in which several children talked about how they wanted to help the Aboriginal People get their rights. After reading this account, a few parents suggested a letter-writing campaign to the Parliament and prime minister, an idea that Krista eagerly took up. One mother, a lawyer, wrote a description of legislation that was currently under consideration and that people could explicitly support. The children, most of the parents, and a number of people from the community joined in and, in the end, over 100 letters, many with poems and colorful drawings, were sent.

Several parents expressed interest in continuing discussions about Aboriginal issues, and the director of the school started a book group for parents and staff that focused on Aboriginal authors. Krista encouraged a few of the most interested parents to become involved in groups supporting Aboriginal rights.

Reflection Questions

1. What was most meaningful to you in Krista's story?
2. How might you apply the strategies that Krista used in your own work?

STRATEGIC PLANNING

As Krista's story illustrates, effective AB/MC work requires learning about children and families in deeper and more complex ways, monitoring their reactions and the ever changing dynamics of the community and the larger society, and developing flexible and creative strategies. This process, which we call strategic planning, consists of the following six steps:

1. *Formulate a specific topic or central question* based on an incident that has occurred in the classroom or children's community or that comes from your own experiences or concerns or those of parents or staff members and that is relevant to one or more of the learning themes described in the Introduction.
2. *Gather and analyze relevant information.* How do children feel about this issue? How does it relate to family background and experiences and the history of and current issues in the commu-

nity? How do families and staff members feel about the issue and what do they know about it?

3. *Use your analysis to generate clear, child-based inquiry questions* on which to build your curriculum.

4. *Choose, create, and implement specific activities* for children, families, staff or a combination of these.

5. *Record responses of children (or families or staff members) and evaluate the activities.* This assessment is child (and adult) specific but can also be used to analyze the curriculum as a whole.

6. *Identify new or deeper ways* to explore the current issue or to choose a new focus, based on what you learned in Step 5. The strategic planning cycle begins again, always building on the previous cycle.

In short, strategic planning for effective AB/MC work calls on teachers to be thoughtful about their choices of specific topics and activities with children, families, and staff/colleagues in order to create curriculum that is relevant and meaningful to a particular setting.

In the following example, teachers in one all-white preschool classroom (primarily 3- and 4-year-olds) created a series of activities based on their observations that the children were avoiding dark colors in their artwork and making disparaging remarks about photographs of darker-skinned people. The teachers decided to create an integrated curriculum that would focus on darkness and lightness in their many forms and expressions and, through these activities, to expose children to new perspectives and to challenge their racialized feelings about darkness and lightness. This project touched on Learning Themes 4 and 5.

> To learn more about why and how the children were avoiding dark colors, the teachers put out markers and paints of many different colors, including black and brown and different skin tones, and closely observed which colors specific children selected and avoided. They also watched how much children played with the darker-skinned dolls versus the lighter-skinned ones. They provided books that depicted children of different racial groups. As much as they could, the teachers unobtrusively listened to children's conversations as they played with the dolls and leafed through the books. When appropriate, teachers would comment or ask questions to encourage children to express their thoughts.
>
> When they pooled their observations, the teachers felt that they had a fairly comprehensive idea about how specific children were thinking and feeling about darkness and lightness as a

physical phenomenon and how they were related to children's early racial conceptions and attitudes.

The teachers knew that the families were not familiar with AB/MC work. Moreover, when the topic had been raised at the initial family-school meeting, a few had expressed reservations. Thus, the teachers felt that talking about colors rather than race per se might provide a better entry point. As part of the information-gathering step, the children interviewed family members about their most and least favorite colors. Parents reported that some of these interviews evolved into interesting conversations about why people like certain colors and why they tend to dislike darker colors.

As the teachers began to sift through the information and make their plans, they reviewed and, when necessary, augmented the resources at the school—art supplies (there was *plenty* of black and brown paint and paper), lighting equipment to do experiments on light and dark, and books and photographs depicting lightness and darkness (including positive images of darkness) and people with different shades of skin color.

From the very beginning of the curriculum project, the teachers worked closely with the director of the school. She committed herself to supporting them and talked about which families might be receptive and which ones more resistant. She also advised them how to avoid some of the problems that had happened in the past (for example, one teacher had been very confrontational with parents, which had resulted in a backlash against all AB/MC activities for a while). The teachers also presented their ideas at the monthly staff meeting. Several colleagues were interested and offered a number of suggestions. The teachers also invited family members to join in a couple of late-afternoon meetings to brainstorm ideas.

The teachers planned the initial activities around the most frequent comments and questions that they had heard from the children during the "investigation" period. The association of darkness and fear had been a common theme, so the teachers decided to start with challenging that link. With the help of several parents, they created activities using the colors brown and black—painting with light colors on brown and black paper, making black play dough, and experimenting with blocking sunlight. They introduced positive images of darkness, such as black and brown puppies, stuffed animals, and the cool shade under a big tree, to counteract children's fearful associations. The teachers and children created a house out of a refrigerator box and painted the inside black and put in lots of soft pillows to make it a restful place.

Finally, as activities and concepts were introduced, teachers observed and documented children's reactions carefully. They quickly discovered that the house was too frightening—the children either avoided it altogether or threatened to put each other into the "scary" house. One of the parents suggested punching a few small holes to let in a bit of light. From that point on the house became a popular spot for children who needed time alone. It also provided opportunities for teachers to talk about how restful and peaceful darkness can be.

As the curriculum developed, the teachers shifted the focus from colors per se to skin colors and race. The children, having spent a lot of time working with black and many shades of brown no longer had an automatic aversion to darker skin but were eager to learn more about why skin colors vary. When they discovered that a new box of markers did not include the colors black and brown (a common occurrence), the children dictated a letter to the manufacturer protesting this choice of colors and its underlying message that black and brown are not appealing.

Reflection Questions

1. How did you feel about the activities described in this story? What questions did they raise for you? Do you see ways that you might be able to adapt them to your classroom?
2. Think of activities that you have done with children. Are there ways that you are already using the strategic planning process?

WORKING WITH ADULT RESISTANCE

Many early childhood professionals feel called to their work because of their comfort and delight in working with children, yet are uneasy about working with adults. However, AB/MC work cannot be done in a vacuum; families and colleagues must be part of the process. If they are not, their misunderstanding or resistance will undermine teachers' efforts. One teacher quotes the phone message she found when she came to work one morning:

> Caitlin came home today all upset because Angela [the teacher] told her that white people are mean to black people. I just want

you to know that I am not paying my money to send my child
to a program where she is learning that all white people are
bad!

Another teacher describes being derailed when she enthusiastically
described her plans for a multicultural workshop, and her colleagues dismissed the idea: "I don't see why we have to do all this diversity stuff. Can't
we just let kids be kids and not bother them with all this depressing information that has nothing to do with their lives?"

Although adult resistance to AB/MC education may feel overwhelming, it can be addressed, and, at least sometimes, turned around. When
teachers are aware of the dynamics underlying resistance, they are able to
generate more effective strategies for working with it.

First, many whites believe that AB/MC education about race and racism is either irrelevant or harmful to their children. They deny or ignore
the systemic racism and white privilege that remains pervasive in the
United States, albeit in more covert or subtle forms than in the past. Some
may be aware of their racial privilege but are invested in denying and pro-
tecting it and so see AB/MC education as threatening. They argue that
strategies used to redress the inequities of racism victimize white people.
They also do not want their children to feel upset about the current consequences of racism; they do not recognize that such obliviousness is a luxury
of white privilege.

Second, white individuals who feel (and in fact may be) economically
disadvantaged may resent AB/MC work because they see it as part of a
pattern in the preferential treatment of people of color, which they blame
for their own economic straits. Teachers working with lower-income white
families need to recognize and acknowledge that these families, in fact, do
not experience many of the privileges racism brings. At the same time,
teachers can talk with individuals about how white poverty and the oppression of people of color are different facets of the same inequitable system; how economic disadvantage does not negate the reality of racial
oppression; and how, by joining forces with people of color, they are better able to effect change.

Finally, one of the most pervasive arguments against AB/MC education is the notion that young children are "color-blind"; that is, they do not
notice racial or other differences among people. This assumption, and the
belief that talking with children about differences leads to prejudice, directly oppose the anti-bias stance, which argues that children develop prejudices because they are living in a racist society. The color-blind position
silences children and adults and invalidates the ongoing racism experienced by people of color. The AB/MC position holds that encouraging

children to talk about race enables them to recognize, explore, and rethink misconceptions and to develop understanding of and comfort with racial diversity. Knowledge about research that documents how many young children absorb messages about race and racism (see Chapters 3 and 7) is an important tool for challenging the color-blind position.

Reflection Questions

1. What reasons have you heard from families or staff for not doing anti-bias education?
2. What expressions of "color blindness" do you see in your own thinking and in others?
3. What are your worst fears about experiencing resistance to AB/MC education from families or colleagues?

KNOWING YOURSELF

Having support for AB/MC work from the other adults in children's lives requires that teachers form caring and collaborative connections among and between staff and families. To do this, you first need to consider your own attitudes and social and professional skills with adults. It is essential to think about how well you empathize with others, connect with people you do not know well or understand deeply, and manage and resolve conflicts about emotional or sensitive issues. The next step is to identify areas where you want to grow and to plan ways to do so. Remember, do not get caught in self-blame or discouragement; what matters is your willingness and efforts to learn. A good way to start is by asking yourself the following questions:

- What are my strengths for working with adults? What are my anxieties or limitations? How can I overcome these and build on my strengths?
- Are there individuals I understand and empathize with more than with others? What accounts for these different responses? Do race, social class, culture, occupation, age, gender, sexual orientation, abilities, religion, or political views play a role?
- When I disagree with someone, how much do I try to understand his/her perspective and find common ground? How concerned am I about "winning" the argument?
- How do I react when racial issues come up in a conversation? Do I feel anxious? Defensive? Do I speak openly, or do I start censoring myself? How do my reactions differ if I am in a group in

which everyone is the same race as I am versus one that is racially diverse?

- What are my hopes for and fears about opening up issues of race and racism with myself, with my family and friends, with colleagues? How can I work with and overcome these fears? Whom can I count on to join me?
- What is my vision of a new white identity that is not based on racial advantage? What would it look like, feel like? How do I think I can live at least parts of this identity in my current life?

The process of self-reflection is a necessity for all effective teaching. It has particular importance, however, when we are teaching material that requires us to grow and learn alongside the children and families to whom we are responsible. In a society that has obscured and hidden the realities of white racial privilege and its effect on the rest of the world, all of us are finding new ways to think and act, learning as we go.

THE ADULT ANTI-RACIST JOURNEY

The literature about the phases of white racial identity development (Derman-Sparks & Phillips, 1997; Helms, 1995; Tatum, 1992) is a useful resource for developing strategies that encourage people to take the next steps on their journey. Although most authors use the term *racial identity development*, we think it is more accurate to describe this process as *anti-racist identity development*.

This journey begins when the silence about whiteness is broken (Tatum, 1992). It is about people recognizing the reality and implications of their white racial identity and undoing their learned racial superiority and entitlement. It is about overcoming fears about losing connections with family, colleagues, and friends because of these choices. However, the anti-racist white journey is also about becoming more whole, healing the wounds of alienation and dehumanization that racism creates, and opening up to the richness of human diversity in our country and world. Thus, the research on white racial identity development, while revealing the challenges of this process, also offers hope and inspiration by demonstrating how people can grow in their self-understanding, learn to manage increasingly complex racial material, and take active responsibility for challenging racism.

As you read the following descriptions of Helms's (1995) phases of white identity development, keep in mind that the anti-racism identity journey is fluid and more a spiral than a ladder. In addition, at any particular point in time, an individual's sense of identity and response to racism are also influenced by social context and the issues that arise. Furthermore, individuals often make detours and get stuck at certain points on the journey, before moving ahead. So avoid pigeonholing yourself or others or expecting that you or anyone else will pass smoothly through these phases.

Precontact Phase

In this phase, individuals are oblivious to or unconcerned about racial issues. Alternatively, they may be confident that racism is a thing of the past or claim that they have no responsibility for what happened before they were alive. Claiming color blindness is also typical of people in the precontact phase. These views usually result in people seeing no need for or value in doing AB/MC education. Some even may proudly identify with their racial and economic entitlement and express little concern about people who are disadvantaged.

> Never in my life have I ever been ashamed of being an upper-class white male. . . . I don't have anything to gain by having Black and white equal. . . . If you're born and you could have your choice of what you wanted to be, white male would probably be that choice, because that is the best thing to be. (quoted in Maher & Tetrault, 1998, p. 138)

Even white people from less economically privileged backgrounds often believe that everyone has an equal opportunity and is responsible for his/her failure or success. As one working-class white man said, "We are all equal, and I feel that . . . I've worked for myself to get to where I am at. . . . If they [people of color] would just really try instead of just hanging out on street corners . . . just kind of milling around doing nothing (Weis, Proweller, & Centrie, 1997, p. 215).

If you are working with colleagues and family members who express these ideas, you might begin to challenge such views by describing research that shows how children are constructing their ideas about race even at very young ages. It is useful to supplement published research with examples of the ideas and attitudes of the children with whom you work. Another strategy is to share short articles that have concrete statistics and examples (such as health and salary information across different racial groups) illustrating the impact of racism and other "isms" on people's lives to help people at this phase begin to see that there is (still!) a problem. Inviting individuals to examine children's storybooks and television programming for stereotypes and misinformation is another way to expose them to the pervasiveness and effects of racism.

Disequilibrium Phase

Some adults may be in the disequilibrium phase, which often occurs when people who have been in denial come to realize that racism is real and pervasive and is affecting their lives. In this phase, people often feel guilty and overwhelmed. *It is essential to help people understand how they were socialized into racism from a very early age and without their personal consent and to assure them that, as adults, they do have the power to change their attitudes and behaviors.* People in the disequilibrium phase benefit from expressing these feelings, but without getting stuck in them, and exploring ways that they can begin to make small changes at home and at school. Invite family members and colleagues to participate in classroom activities and think about how they might adapt them to their particular home or classroom situation. Participating in small, relatively nonthreatening anti-bias actions (writing to publishers or television producers about stereotypes or omissions in their materials and programs or modifying school forms to make them more inclusive, for example, changing *father* and *mother* to *parent/guardian*) may help people see that they have the power to make a difference. They can direct their guilt and discomfort toward a positive outcome, rather than simply being paralyzed by them.

Reintegration Phase

Some, but not all, whites may attempt to get away from the uncomfortable realizations and feelings of the disequilibrium phase by "reintegrating" into their oblivion about race and refusing to participate in any discussions about racial issues. People in this phase may assume that they already know all they need to know about race and so do not need to discuss it again. They rationalize that any race-related inequities are the fault of people of color and deride and resent efforts (including the current conversation) that attempt to address them ("Yeah, yeah, I used to believe all that bleeding-heart stuff—but now I realize that some people are just lazy. Why should they get all that preferential treatment for jobs and schools?")

Listening to individuals' fears and frustrations may help them to identify where these feelings come from and possibly rethink them. Initially talking about issues that are meaningful to them (such as feeling threatened by possible layoffs at their workplace) can provide an entry point for considering inequities in other realms. Fostering relationships between individuals in the precontact and reintegration phases with individuals who are supportive of exploring the issues of AB/MC work (pairing family members together on field trips or encouraging particular staff members to work together on a project) is another way to support and encourage people to move beyond this phase.

Pseudoindependent Phase

As a consequence of experiences that compel them to continue their journeys toward a more complete understanding of racism, many whites enter what Helms calls the pseudoindependent phase. Individuals begin to recognize and challenge the prevailing assumptions about white superiority and develop an intellectual commitment to anti-racist work. This phase is an important step forward, but not yet sufficient. While people now begin, with good intentions, to take actions to challenge racism, they often unintentionally perpetuate the power relationships that they want to change. They may also begin to reject their whiteness and seek out relationships with people of color to bolster their identities as "good whites." At this point, people benefit from learning about institutional racism in more depth and, in particular, how socialization into white privilege affects psychology and behavior. Support groups where people can empathetically give one another feedback about ways they are acting out their internalized white superiority and brainstorm alternative ways of acting can be very growth producing.

Immersion/Emersion Phase

For people in this phase, understanding how racism operates is empowering because it provides a framework for identifying what needs to be changed in society, as well as in oneself. Making connections between racism and other forms of systemic advantage and disadvantage (sexism, heterosexism, classism, and ableism) also strengthens people's knowledge and helps them to understand the overall structure of inequities. In the immersion/emersion phase, stories about other whites who have struggled with their own racism and have participated in anti-racist movements are a source of encouragement and positive role models (Tatum, 1999; see also Appendix C in the present book; Aptheker, 1993; Brown, 2002; Curry et al., 2000; Virginia Dorr's biography in Colby & Damon, 1992; Howard, 1999; McIntyre, 1997; Stalvey, 1989; Zinn, 1995). These stories can help whites reclaim the history of white dissent and struggle for justice that has often been omitted or glossed over in history books and integrate this history into their construction of a "new white" identity.

Autonomy Phase

In this phase of anti-racist identity development, an individual has a clear, positive sense of him/herself as a white person within a social-political context and actively participates in anti-racist, social justice movements. Now, people often feel that engaging in anti-racism work is not a choice but a reflection of one's core identity and integrity (Derman-Sparks & Phillips, 1997). While Helms uses the term *autonomy* for this phase, thereby capturing the choice to think independently about what the dominant culture has taught, whites in this phase no longer see themselves as separate individuals. Rather, they recognize that their future is integrally connected to what happens to the rest of the human family.

Autonomy is the last phase that Helms identifies, but the anti-racist white identity journey is always a work in progress. So the meaning of *last* as *lasting* is perhaps the more relevant. Even those who have been engaged in anti-racism work for years are always learning and growing.

Reflection Questions

1. What phases best represent your own history and growth? Those of your friends and colleagues?
2. How might you use this information about anti-racist identity phases for your own growth and for working with other adults?

In sum, doing AB/MC education means seeing its hopeful possibilities as well as meeting its challenges. The work calls on us to be persistent yet strategic, passionate yet thoughtful, proactive yet patient. It calls for our creativity as well as our knowledge. Ultimately, it requires us to have faith that change can and will happen.

Identity and Racism

Part I (Chapters 2, 3, 4, and 5) turns the spotlight on white identity. In Chapter 2 we look at the historic creation and evolution of whiteness in the United States. In Chapter 3 we review research about how children develop white identities and learn racism's codes of power. In Chapter 4 we discuss how to implement the first three learning themes with children and in Chapter 5 how to engage families and staff. Part I concludes with Episode I of "A Tale of Two Centers," which illustrates how the ideas in Chapters 4 and 5 might be implemented in two different early childhood programs.

CHAPTER 2

A Short History of White Racism in the United States

> Whiteness is a concept, an ideology, which holds tremendous power over our lives and, in turn, over the lives of people of color. . . . [It] is an arbitrary category that overrides our individual personalities . . . [and] governs our day-to-day lives just as much as being a person of color does.
>
> —Paul Kivel, *Uprooting Racism: How White People Can Work for Racial Justice*

Despite many decades of reform, systemic racism continues to fragment our country and wound us all. In this chapter we will discuss the roots and history of racism and how it affects our welfare and national identity. This material may sometimes seem abstract and distant in terms of time and place, but to design and implement curriculum to counteract racism, teachers need to understand how it became woven into our social and political structures. To help you see the connections between this material and your own work, we have included reflection questions after each major section.

ROOTS AND HISTORY OF RACISM

Racism embodies a belief that within the human species, biological "racial" differences exist and some racial groups are superior to others. This concept was deeply rooted in European ideologies (in the British view of the Irish as savages, in the exclusion of Jewish people from many countries). When European colonizers came to the Americas, their assumptions about racial superiority enabled them to justify the genocide and enslavement of indigenous people and the kidnapping and enslavement of African people. Their actions were supported by many "scientific" and popular writings in the 18th, 19th, and early 20th centuries that "proved" that Europeans, particularly northern Europeans, were a superior race (C. S. Brown, 2002).

In the 20th century these views began to be challenged as scientific evidence increasingly made clear that there was no valid genetic basis for distinguishing racial groups. In fact, decades of genetic research and, most recently, the Human Genome Project, have shown that there is more within-race than between-race variability (C. S. Brown, 2002).

Nevertheless, race is, and has always been, a social-political construct masquerading as biological fact. It has been defined and redefined by social, economic, and political forces (Omi & Winant, 1986) in ways that have reflected the interests and beliefs of those in power. Despite its lack of validity, this construct underlies a system of racial advantage and disadvantage and continues to influence the life prospects of all Americans—both those who are viewed as racially superior and those who are targets of racial discrimination.

The idea that racism is an intentionally created and maintained system that advantages European Americans is a difficult one for white people to swallow. Most would prefer to maintain the status quo and "help" the disadvantaged rather than recognize and challenge their own racial power and privilege (Tatum, 1997). Accepting this definition of racism requires whites to face the fact that eliminating racism does not mean simply unlearning individual prejudice. Rather, it requires transforming economic and political systems and structures, giving up power, and equitably sharing resources.

Racism and Entitlement

Many analyses of racism focus on its negative effects on people of color and ignore the notion of "whiteness" that is imbedded in racial hierarchies. However, assumptions about racial inferiority could not exist without the concept of superiority. "Ideological racism includes strongly positive images of the white self as well as strongly negative images of the racial 'others'" (Feagin, 2000, p. 33). These beliefs, in turn, engender a sense of entitlement, which is the core of the social-political construct of whiteness.

> When people grow up in a society where, despite rhetoric about equal opportunity, they are given more access to power, status, goods and services, they will come to think that they or their group is superior and that they deserve more than others. And they may become upset, bitter, and resentful if they don't receive what they see as their due. In fact,

when they are treated the same or like everyone else, because of their expectations they will perceive themselves to be victimized or to be at a disadvantage, simply because they have lost the unacknowledged advantage they had (Kivel, 2002, p. 42).

This sense of entitlement is self-perpetuating because many white individuals believe that their financial and professional successes are the results of their own efforts and ignore the fact that they have also benefited from their racial advantage (Tatum, 1997). These assumptions are supported by the European American cultural orientation toward individualism and competition that reflect the Founding Fathers' Enlightenment philosophies and Protestant beliefs that God materially rewards those who deserve it.

The Definitions and Contradictions of Whiteness

For the earliest European settlers, it was necessary to define who was and was not white, in order to endow whiteness with power and privilege, which were not to be shared with other "races." Furthermore, it was necessary to distinguish the white "race" from the "race" of enslaved Africans and their offspring, to define and treat them as property and therefore as not qualified to receive any of the legal benefits of the new United States (the right to their children, the right to vote). In contrast to Africans, indentured servants from Europe were able to earn their freedom and subsequently gain the legal and economic advantages (owning and inheriting property, voting, getting an education, being legally protected by due process) enjoyed by the dominant group. As Eric Dyson's explains, "Only when black bodies—through slavery on to the present—have existed on American terrain has whiteness been constituted as an idea and, indeed, an identity-based reality" (cited in Chennault, 1998, p. 300).

The parameters of whiteness, however, have not remained constant. Debates about which ethnic groups are white have erupted on numerous occasions. The outcomes of these controversies were not simply academic; they affected the civil status, rights, and economic viability of each group. The determination of European Americans to maintain control often resulted in convoluted and contradictory legal reasoning. For example, in 1923 the U.S. Supreme Court denied citizenship to a Japanese resident on the grounds that notwithstanding his white skin, he did not have Caucasian features. Three months later the Court denied Indian immigrants citizenship because, although they had Caucasian features, they had dark skin (Foley, 2002).

Wealth and having connections with the European American establishment played a role in these legal proceedings. In California in the mid-1880s, Mexicans who were wealthy landowners and business partners with whites were legally designated as white, whereas poor Mexicans and Chinese laborers were categorized as nonwhite, on a par with blacks and Indians (Kivel, 2002).

The "Whitening" of European Immigrants

During the great waves of immigration from southern and eastern Europe in the late 19th century, scholars and politicians in the United States "discovered" that "Europe had inferior and superior races" (Brodkin, 2002, p. 36). Earlier, European immigrants from different countries had been assimilated into Anglo-American communities. When 23 million immigrants arrived, however, they were too numerous to blend in, and cities became distinctly more ethnic. Not surprisingly, wealthy white Protestants who had come from northwestern Europe were the most threatened, and they regarded this influx as "race suicide" (p. 37).

Similar to the "scientific" justifications for slavery that had appeared in the 18th and 19th centuries, tests were created in the early 20th century to distinguish superior "Nordics" from inferior "Alpines," "Mediterraneans," and "Jews." "By the 1920s, scientific racism sanctified the notion that real Americans were white and real whites came from northwest Europe" (Brodkin, 2002, p. 38). However, even these categories embodied many contradictions. For example, the courts consistently ruled that Finns, who were ethnically Nordic, were not white, because they occupied the lowest-paid and riskiest mining and lumbering jobs in the Upper Midwest (Kivel, 2002).

New "nonwhite" European immigrants were scorned and marginalized and were often the target of racial violence (such as lynching and race riots); they quickly learned that to be American meant becoming "white" (Barrett & Roediger, 2002). The centrality of whiteness is illustrated in the histories of how European immigrants from various nationalities and ethnicities bought into the myth of white supremacy to legitimize their membership in the dominant group and their claims to economic privilege (Roediger, 2005). Becoming white, as Toni Morrison writes, required that "a hostile posture toward resident blacks must be struck at the Americanizing door before it will open" (cited in Foley, 2002, p. 55). Ignatiev (1995) describes how Irish immigrants, who experienced great discrimination from Anglo-Americans and initially identified with their black coworkers, became hostile to black people as they learned the advantages of being white. Likewise, Brodkin (2002) traces the history of how Jewish people in the United States also became "white." This pressure to distinguish and distance oneself from African and Asian Americans sowed seeds of the intransigent racism that has undermined the unity and effectiveness of the labor movement and has deeply imbedded a racist ideology into our national psyche.

Today, despite changing demographics that predict that whites will make up only half the U.S. population by 2050, "the term 'American' still means 'white'—at least for the majority of white Americas, and probably for most people across the globe" (Feagin, 2000, p. 99). This norm of "whiteness" is simply assumed, rarely mentioned, and reinforced in subtle ways. We only have to recall that the "race" or ethnicity of people of color is often mentioned in the media, while the "race" of white people is almost never identified.

Reflection Questions

1. What do you know about your own extended family's history that relates to this account of racism and whiteness? What types of discrimination or privilege did your ancestors experience?
2. How does your extended family's history affect your understanding of who you are?
3. How did you experience the invisible norm of whiteness when you were growing up? How do you see it expressed in your community and work?

CONTEMPORARY WHITE RACISM

White people today often assume that white dominance and racism are a thing of the past thanks to the civil rights movement and subsequent legislation (Lipsitz, 2002). As one white teacher who grew up in rural Vermont said, "The adults in my life believed, and told me, that racism had ended with the civil rights movement. . . . Segregation was presented as something that happened down South but would never occur where we lived" (Alvarado et al., 1999). In fact, many whites express annoyance that they have to learn or feel guilty about slavery and more recent racial discrimination. Some complain that now *they* are the victims of anger, on the part of black people, or of affirmative action policies (Lipsitz, 2002). People of color, in turn, often resent whites' assertions that racial discrimination no longer exists and whites' unwillingness to consider the cumulative effects of past and current exclusion.

While the civil rights movement of the late 1950s and the 1960s did end the system of legal segregation, institutional racism still exists, albeit in more subtle forms. "Today, the color-blind ideology provides a veneer of liberality which covers up continuing racist thought and practice that is often less overt and more disguised" (Feagin, 2000, p. 93). For example, recent surveys have shown that a majority of white Americans feel that racial discrimination is no longer a problem. However, people of color disagree (Bush, 2004; Feagin, 2000). Moreover, many whites, despite their assumptions that racism is a thing of the past, still harbor many racist views. An Anti-Defamation League survey asked whites whether they agreed with one or more anti-black views (for instance blacks "have less native intelligence than people of other races"). Three-quarters of the whites agreed with one or more of the statements, more than half agreed with two or more, and almost a third agreed with four or more (cited in Feagin, 2000, p. 109, n. 11).

Furthermore, although mainstream politicians and institutions avoid openly racist comments and practices, many white-supremacist groups vociferously advocate the genocide of people of color. The groups continue to exist and exert influence, especially on whites who feel disadvantaged by the system and are eager to blame their frustrations on vulnerable scapegoats. These groups are considered "fringe," but their hatred and violence still filter into all aspects of our society and pose a threat to people of color and to whites who are fighting for social justice. Because we do not expect that anyone from these groups would read this book, we are not addressing the issue of the groups per se. However, we do recognize that the drumbeat of racial hatred still beats in our country and may be influencing the views of more moderate people.

Effects of Systemic Racial Advantage and Disadvantage

Economic and other quality-of-life statistics give clear evidence of how racial advantage and disadvantage continue to reverberate in the country. One percent of the U.S. population owns 47% of the country's net financial wealth. Of this group, the overwhelming number is white (Kivel, 2004). Moreover, a vast disparity exists between the highest and lowest incomes: In 2002 the income of the top 20% accounted for 50% of the total U.S. income, while the income of the bottom 20% accounted for 3.5% of the total U.S. income (Strope, 2004). People of color are disproportionately represented in the later group (Kivel, 2004), as the proportion of people of color living in poverty is almost 4 times higher than it is for white people. When educational backgrounds are the same, the unemployment rate for whites is one-third of that for African Americans and one-half of that for Latino Americans (Heinz, Folbre, & The Center for Popular Economics, 2000). These economic disparities affect all aspects of quality of life for children, as the Children's Defense Fund's annual report (2005), has documented for many years. Indicator after indicator demonstrate that white families enjoy higher incomes, longer life spans, better health care, more education, and better-serviced neighborhoods.

Furthermore, many institutions have continued to be racially divided. Although school segregation was legally ended 50 years ago by the landmark Supreme Court decision *Brown v. Board of Education*, it not only persists, but rose during the 1990s (Tatum, 1997). The most segregated schools are those that African American and Latino children attend. Moreover, these schools also tend to have a larger percentage of children from poor families, whereas 96% of white schools have middle-class majorities (Tatum, 1997). Kozol (1991) has graphically described how educational resources and opportunities are distributed along racial lines.

These patterns also emerge in early childhood settings. Because most programs are privately funded, many are segregated by income and therefore by race. Affluent families either employ nannies or send their children to schools with high tuition costs; working-class and poor families use federally funded services such as Head Start or rely on family members or neighbors for child care; and middle-class families struggle to find child care that they can afford. Racial hierarchies often exist within child-care centers and schools; the custodial and paraprofessional staff are likely to be people of color, whereas teachers and, in particular, directors and principals are usually white.

On a personal level, most whites are struggling with their daily lives; they do not feel that they are dominating anyone and may vigorously deny the reality of white advantage. But the reality is that in the United States and elsewhere, white people still benefit from a system of unearned racial privilege (McIntosh, 1995; Tatum, 1992), while people from other racial groups suffer undeserved racial penalties (Howard, 1999). Whiteness is the invisible norm. Consequently, all whites in the United States, be they male or female, rich or poor, live in a protective racial bubble that gives them a sense of belonging and access to resources that are denied people of color; regardless of personal intentions, lifestyles, or political and social beliefs, all whites must confront the fact that they benefit from belonging to the group that currently dominates and defines the national and global economic, cultural, and political infrastructures

Diversity Among Whites

Although the social umbrella of whiteness benefits all people allowed under it, regardless of national or ethnic background, whites are not homogeneous. Ranged against the privileges of whiteness is an array of ethnic groups with different histories, languages, cultures, and power relationships vis-à-vis other "white" groups in the United States.

Historically, upper-class settlers emigrating from England in the 17th and 18th centuries became the most privileged group. "Boston Brahmins,"

New York merchants, and Southern plantation owners dominated the early cultural and political history of this country. Many of their descendents still hold sway in financial, political, and educational institutions. By contrast poor English, Irish, and Scottish families who arrived at about the same time, settling in isolated communities in the Appalachian Mountains, and their descendants have been the targets of ridicule and discrimination for centuries, giving rise to derogatory remarks about "hillbillies" and "rednecks."

Today, the material advantages of being white have yet to be equally distributed. Lower-income whites do not experience the full benefits of white privilege accorded their more affluent counterparts. White families from a range of ethnic groups suffer chronic severe poverty. As with other racial groups, economic status is tied to gender and to age, with women, children, and the elderly more often living in poverty than adult nonelderly males.

Thus, some whites dismiss the notion that they are privileged. Yet even the poorest white person does not suffer the added pressures of racial discrimination that shape the lives and prospects of people of color, even though they lead lives different from middle-class and wealthy whites.

Within ethnic and social-class groups, individual whites respond to the realities of racism in different ways. Some may feel powerless and resent programs that they perceive as giving people of color unfair advantage. Others may be more secure in their livelihoods but choose to ignore or justify the plight of groups that suffer from racism. Still others may challenge the existing racially based power structure by engaging in multicultural and social-justice work. However, even those who vigorously disagree with the system of racial privilege may not be able to truly give up their advantages or radically challenge the status quo (Thomas, 1996).

Reflection Questions

1. What types of economic advantages or disadvantages did your ancestors have? How have those shaped your family's views about other groups?
2. How has contemporary racism affected your life? What benefits or disadvantages have you experienced?
3. How have your position in society and your experiences influenced your views of racism?

COSTS OF RACISM TO WHITES

Despite their overall material advantage, whites also are negatively affected by racism. The lower wages of people of color are always an available weapon to undermine the wages of white workers (Roediger, 1991). The women's movement, from its early days of fighting for the vote, has been undercut by its internal racism, affecting progress for women of all backgrounds (Davis, 1983). Tatum (1997) points out how racism undermines the whole economy:

> Whether one looks at productivity lowered by racial tensions in the workplace, or real estate equity lost through housing discrimination, or the tax revenue lost in underemployed communities of color, or the high cost of warehousing human talent in prison, the economic costs of racism are real and measurable. (p. 140)

Racism has had a significant impact on the cultural and linguistic heritage of European ethnic groups (Brodkin, 2002; Gossett, 1963; Ignatiev, 1991). Many immigrant groups, especially in the first half of the 20th century, went to great lengths to maintain their languages and cultures, through, for example, language schools and community cultural organizations. However, these efforts were abandoned as many individuals chose to give up their traditions in order to "become white" and to assimilate into the dominant, primarily Anglo-American, culture. While this new American culture offered whites some cultural freedoms that did not exist in their traditional cultures, it also erased important parts of family history. Not surprisingly, many white Americans deny having a specific ethnic heritage, preferring to see themselves as an amalgam. Some even express regret about "not having any culture." In essence, the majority of whites have lost their own ethnic cultures and histories in order to gain the privileges of whiteness (Kivel, 2002).

Whites have paid a price for benefiting from racism's system of advantage, although not nearly as high a price as paid by people of color. However, most whites—unlike people of color—are unaware of the price they pay. To fully understand the dynamics of racism and to challenge them, we must face both the advantages and the costs racism brings to white people, as well as the disadvantages racism brings to people of color.

Reflection Questions

1. How have you experienced the "cost of racism"?
2. How do you see white families that you work with experiencing the "cost of racism"?

In sum, whiteness is a many faceted and changing phenomenon that perpetuates a racial hierarchy and protects the power of white people. It is a powerful fiction with wide-ranging effects on the lives of all people of color. Although there are no natural or essential qualities or characteristics of whiteness, or of white people, "it is not an easy fiction to let go of" (Kivel, 2000, p. 23). Most whites, even those who disagree with racist practices, hold unconscious beliefs that they are inherently superior and deserve to be in power. As we embark on our journey to examine the racism in our lives and its effects on children and the broader community, we need to recognize how racial categories and advantages and disadvantages are integrated into identities of all people. In the following chapter we will talk about how white racial identities and entitlement are woven into children's lives from an early age.

FOR FURTHER READING

Barndt, J. (1991). *Dismantling racism: The continuing challenge to white America*. Minneapolis: Augsberg.

Kivel, P. (2002). *Uprooting racism: How white people can work for racial justice* (2nd ed). British Columbia, Canada: New Society.

Roediger, D. (2005). *Working toward whiteness: How America's immigrants became white*. New York: Basic Books.

Sleeter, C. (2001). *Culture, difference, and power*. [CD-ROM]. New York: Teachers College Press.

Wise, T. (2005). *White like me: Reflections on race from a privileged son*. New York: Soft Skull Press.

CHAPTER 3

How Children Construct White Identities

"Mommy, I'm really glad that I'm white," a 4-year-old child remarked to his mother, who was driving him home from his preschool, which maintains two separate programs, one for affluent, mostly white children, and a subsidized one for low-income children, mostly of color.

As this quotation illustrates, children readily notice, absorb, and behaviorally reflect the patterns of racial and economic privilege that permeate their environments. To counteract these influences and to nurture anti-racist identities requires an understanding of racial and economic socialization. In this chapter, we will review the research on white children's racial socialization and identity development and how these early developments play out in adulthood. We will also talk about how economic disparities and consumerism support children's notions of white racial superiority and how to counter those trends by creating caring communities. As we did in the preceeding chapter, we will include reflection questions at the end of each section to encourage you to see how this information is pertinent to your own life and work.

DEVELOPING WHITE RACIAL-GROUP IDENTITY

A body of research about children and race, from the 1950s on (e.g., Clark, 1963; Goodman, 1952; Radke & Trager, 1950), tells us that children begin to construct their ideas about race and racism very early. The research has focused primarily on white children's attitudes toward other groups. Consequently, we know less about how white children form their racial/ethnic/cultural identities and adjust to white privilege. However, some evidence can be gleaned from 6 decades of research.

Learning About the Power Codes of Race

Many early studies found that European American children never expressed a wish to be black, while African American children frequently either wished to be or believed that they were white (e.g., Clark & Clark, 1947; Morland, 1962; Radke & Trager, 1950). Researchers at that time interpreted these findings as an indication of the negative effect of racism on black children's sense of self. This finding was presented as one of the arguments in favor of integrating schools in *Brown v. Board of Education* in 1954. Interestingly, the recurring pattern of white children's strong preference for own-race people was *not* seen as problematic, reflecting the widely held assumption that integration meant that blacks should adapt to white society, not vice versa.

Many studies over the decades have revealed that young white children readily identify themselves by race (e.g., Clark & Clark, 1947; Goodman, 1952; Katz, 1976; Porter, 1971; Ramsey, 1991b; Ramsey & Myers, 1990). MacNaughton (2004) found that Anglo-Australian preschoolers consistently used whiteness as a category when deciding which doll looked most like them and, in fact, used race more than gender in these selections.

Cross's (1991) distinction between personal identity (PI) and reference-group orientation (RGO) may help to explain the apparent white preference of both white and black children. PI encompasses children's thinking/feelings about their personal abilities and self-worth. RGO reflects children's awareness, understanding, and feelings about their racial/ethnic group. According to Cross, immediate experiences with family and friends shape the PI, whereas the larger society's values and behaviors influence the RGO. Thus, children of color may experience conflicts between their positive personal identities and negative societal messages about their group and, at some level, wish to be white. In contrast, white children receive a barrage of messages from the larger social environment that reinforce positive RGOs as well as positive PIs. In this way, a sense of racial superiority becomes imbedded in white children's racial identities.

This sense of white superiority and a knowledge of racial power codes appear to develop early in life. After observing preschoolers' conversations and play in a racially diverse preschool for a year, Van Ausdale and Feagin (2001) concluded:

> Young children quickly learn the racial-ethnic identities and role performances of the larger society. . . . As white children grow up they learn, develop, and perform the meanings associated with the white identity-role. Black children and other children of color often must cope with

the subordinating expectations imposed on them [by white children], expectations that they may accept or resist. (p. 182)

The authors cite a number of incidents to support their conclusion that white preschool children do incorporate a sense of white superiority in their early identities. For example, one 4-year-old white child who noticed that she was darker than her two white companions asked worriedly, "Does that mean that I'm not white anymore?" and repeatedly asked for reassurance that she was still white, apparently concerned about the consequences of being seen as not white (p. 48).

White children learn that whiteness is regarded as "normal" and characteristics of other racial groups as deviant or abnormal. Ramsey (1982) found that virtually all the 4- and 5-year-olds (both black and white) whom she interviewed believed that everyone was inherently white and that black people had been painted, sunburned, or dirtied. These assumptions may be based on young children's incorrect "theory-making," yet if they are not challenged, they may become the foundation for the ideology that whiteness is normal, natural, and superior.

Further, Van Ausdale and Feagin (2001) documented examples of white children equating whiteness with being an American (two white girls told an Asian boy that he did not "look like an American" [p. 102]). Research in Australia has revealed similar ideas among young white children. Glover (1996) describes a white 5-year-old's insistence that an Aboriginal student teacher must come from another country because "you've got brown skin," despite the student teacher's explanation to the contrary (p. 4). MacNaughton (2004) found that many of the Anglo-Australian preschoolers she studied believed that "being Australian meant having 'white' skin" (p. 69).

The Costs of Racial-Power Codes for White Children

While white children ultimately gain much from being in the dominant group, several writers have identified ways that racism potentially harms young white children's developing sense of self, mental and moral health, and ability to function effectively in a diverse world. Trager and Radke Yarrow (1952) noted that white third graders already knew how to be polite about race relations even though they really thought otherwise. Kutner (1985) described how internalizing white superiority negatively affects children's ability to think critically. Smith (1962) used her own life history to analyze how white children learn how to split their minds from their feelings in the process of learning what it means to be white. In *Children of Privilege*, Robert Coles (1977) wrote about the perils of the dynamic he termed "entitlement," the belief that the world owes one whatever one wants.

Clark (1963) argued that growing up in world of contradictions between the professed goals of equality and democracy and the pressures to violate them by acting on racial prejudice creates moral conflicts and guilt for white children. Furthermore, white children "are being given a distorted perception of reality and of themselves, and are being taught to gain personal status in unrealistic ways" (p. 81). By basing their identities on a sense of racial superiority, white children are at risk for developing overblown, yet fragile, identities instead of developing a solid sense of self based on their real interests, connections to people, and contributions to the community.

How Children Become Socialized into Racism

Children absorb beliefs about white superiority from different sources. The contradictions between the reality of racial inequality and the myth of equal opportunity have been imbedded in the economic, political, and social structures of the United States for the past 400 years and are expressed in many ways. For example, the media regularly conveys positive images of powerful, wealthy, attractive, and "deserving" whites (political leaders, CEOs, news commentators, beauty queens) and negative or limited images of people of color (in stories about crime or poverty and in comedies and music based on racial stereotypes). Children watch and absorb these images, which then become "truths" for them. In their communities children observe power differentials every day, noticing which racial groups live in more and less affluent neighborhoods and who has authority in schools and other institutions. Children who are white absorb further intentional and unintentional messages about race from the significant people in their lives. They may sense their white parents' discomfort in neighborhoods of color; take for granted that only white people live on their street or are friends of their family; learn that the real authority in the classroom is the white teacher, not the Latina aide; and notice at the clinic that the white doctor, not the African American nurse, is in charge.

Another look into influences on children's socialization into whiteness comes from white adults' autobiographic literature and oral stories. Many such adults describe growing up in racially and economically isolated communities, unaware of the racism affecting anyone's life. If they learned about racism from their families, they most likely heard not that it was a system of institutionalized advantage but rather that it consisted of individual acts of bigotry, such as cross burnings. One white teacher recalled that as a child, she "was taught that it was possible for individuals to display bigoted behavior, and of course this was not okay." However, "the idea of institutional racism, even as a thing of the past, was never explored" (Beth Wallace, quoted in Alvarado et al., 1999, p. 133). Another example comes from a white student in one of Tatum's (1992) college classes: "I thought that the people who are racist or subjected to racial stereotypes were found only in small pockets of the U.S., such as the South" (p. 6).

In her work with white teachers, Thomas (2005) found that most attested to being "held back from the kind of questioning and experimenting that children need to do in order to understand a complex issue like race." Thomas (2005) described two cases:

> When T asked about race her parents told her "We don't talk about these things in our family." R's family rarely discussed race. She said, "If they aren't in your life, what's there to talk about?" (p. 1)

After interviewing a number of white teachers, Thomas concluded:

> Given the way that many of us who are White were raised, sometimes I think it's a miracle we can even say the words "race" or "racism." Few of us encountered adults who were interested or pleased with our explorations around race or racism. (p. 2)

As they experience these realities, children construct their ideas about the world. According to Vygotsky (1978) children's learning is a social process that occurs in particular social contexts that reflect the beliefs and politics of the adults around them. At the same time, children do not merely imitate adults; they "actively reshape, blend, and synthesize elements of the preexisting patterns found around them—in families, other social settings, and the mass media" (Van Ausdale & Feagin, 2001, p. 20). Children's evolving cognitive and social-emotional capacities also influence how children make sense of what they see, hear, and do. Thus, each child has a unique interpretation of the world that affects his or her views and receptiveness to AB/MC education.

Reflection Questions

1. What do you recall learning about race as a child? What messages were conveyed by the media? By your parents? Peers? Community members? Were there contradictions between what people said and did?
2. What messages about race do you see children in your program learning from the media, community, and personal relationships?

3. Do you recall any childhood incidents when you felt "silenced" about race? How did that feel? What assumptions did you make as a result?
4. Do you see ways that the children in your program are being silenced about race?

THE INTERACTION OF RACE AND SOCIAL CLASS

A sense of racial superiority is often bolstered by economic disparities among racial groups. As we discussed in Chapter 2, whites are dispro-portionately represented in affluent groups and high-status jobs, and people of color are more often poor and work in low-paying jobs. Thus, as children grow up, they daily witness how social class differences align with race.

As with racial ideologies, economic theories and reality are also fraught with contradictions and ambiguities. Embedded in our national culture is a set of myths about equal economic opportunity and access. At the core is the belief that *all* people who work hard will have access to well-paying jobs and financial abundance. Yet a web of national policies and institu-tional structures consistently favors the wealthy over the poor (e.g., tax codes, banking and bankruptcy laws, minimum wages, the legal system). The effects of Hurricane Katrina, which hit New Orleans and the Gulf Coast as we were working on the final phases of this book, vividly revealed the reality of socio-economic inequities in our country and the policies that perpetuate these disparities. For example, as the country was shocked by the terrible pictures of poor people suffering in the New Orleans Super-dome, the federal administration waived a law that guarantees a minimum wage for employees of federal contractors. This action means that compa-nies can pay even lower wages to the working people. Another example is the tax breaks for the wealthiest people and large corporations in our coun-try that require that middle- and working-class families bear the burden of making up for lost tax revenues. The gap between affluent and poor families is obvious in the vast disparities between schools in wealthy and low-income neighborhoods. These "savage inequalities" (Kozol, 1991) create unequal educational opportunities from the very beginning of children's lives.

However, these realities of systemic disadvantage are largely ignored in our educational system and in most of the media. As a result, wealthy individuals are celebrated as hard workers who deserve their financial success, while poor families often are disparaged and blamed for their poverty.

How Children Learn About Social Class

How and what children learn about social class differences is, in part, influenced by the relative affluence of their families. Many children of white upper-middle-class and wealthy families have nannies, who often are women of color and in many cases recent immigrants. Such children experience the confluence of race, wealth, and power every moment of their early lives. When they get older and enter the wider world, these same children see people who look and talk like them occupying positions of wealth and power (politicians, news anchors, school principals, executives) and those who look different working in subordinate positions (service workers, custodians). As they hear adults talk and begin to experience the rewards of achievement in school, they absorb the message that they deserve unlimited access to resources.

White children who live in low-income families absorb the messages of wealth and entitlement from a different perspective. Although they physically look like the children in the white wealthy families they see in the media, they learn early on that their families cannot get them all the latest toys or name-brand clothes that they constantly see on television. They may be teased and shamed by wealthier children. They rarely see families like theirs on television or in children's books. Consequently, white children from lower-income families are at risk of developing a sense of failure and shame about their families and, by extension, about themselves. These feelings may evolve into resentment, later predisposing them to buy into the overtly racist ideologies that blame people of color for the poverty of white people, rather than prompting them to look to the economic system itself.

Images of race and social class are further entangled by television shows and movies (geared to teens but frequently watched by younger children) that display the opulent lifestyles of sports and popular music stars. Often they include stories about people of color, who represent a tiny fraction of people in these communities. These images in turn obscure the economic disadvantages of people of color, often leading children to assume that, as one white child put it, "black people have all the fancy houses and cool cars." This obfuscation reassures white people that economic discrimination along racial lines does not exist. Moreover, it can foster white resentment and assumptions that any economic success on the part of people of color comes at the expense of white success.

Children's understanding of social class changes as they grow up (Leahy, 1983). Young elementary school children are likely to both describe and explain poverty and wealth in observable concrete terms, such as number of possessions and type of residence. When they are around

10 years of age, children begin to refer to psychological traits, such as motivation, in their explanations of why people are in different circumstances. During childhood and adolescence, children increasingly make the connection between having a job and getting money; and they are more aware of the status and financial benefits associated with specific occupations (Furnham & Stacey, 1991). Finally, adolescents are capable of seeing the role of the social and economic structure in the unequal distribution of wealth (Leahy, 1983). However, even as they are learning about the economic system, children are increasingly caught up in the underlying contradiction between the ideal of equality versus the realities of economic discrimination, competitiveness, and individualism, which inevitably result in inequality.

Young children are beginning to develop a sense of fairness and to notice inequities (Damon, 1980). When asked if it is fair that some people have more money than others, some preschoolers say that it is not fair and suggest that the rich should share with poor people (Ramsey, 1991c). Leahy (1983) and Furby (1979) found that elementary school children advocated equalizing the wealth between rich and poor. However, older children and adolescents, who supposedly had a more comprehensive awareness of the economy, were more likely to justify inequalities by claiming that poor people get what they deserve ("They didn't work hard enough") (Chafel, 1997; Leahy, 1990). Children and adolescents from "working poor" families may succumb to the power of that myth and feel confused and disturbed about their families, who work very hard and yet still have little income. This tendency to blame the poor for their plight reinforces the notion that the wealthy deserve their affluence.

Reflection Questions

1. What do you recall learning or thinking about social-class differences as a child? How did you feel about poor people? Rich people?
2. What obvious and subtle messages about social class do you see in the media?
3. How do social-class differences influence your day-to-day interactions with people at work?

THE EFFECTS OF CONSUMERISM

The effects of economic disparities have been aggravated by the explosive growth of consumerism in the past 3 decades. Children's worlds today are saturated with consumerist messages claiming that purchasing power brings happiness and therefore everyone should buy, buy, buy. Children watch hours of television programs that contain hundreds of overt and covert commercials. They also frequently accompany parents on shopping trips, viewing aisle after aisle filled with enticing objects packaged and presented to elicit children's desire to have them. A subtext of these messages is that satisfying a never ending desire to own new items takes priority over other considerations, such as the needs of other people in the family, environmental sustainability, or equitable distribution of resources.

Consumerism affects children's priorities in ways that undermine the development of authentic identity and the ability to connect with other people (Kline, 1993). First, children learn to relate to physical objects, especially toys and clothes, in terms of *getting* and *having* instead of *using* and *enjoying*. Second, children learn to identify themselves as consumers and owners, not as creators or contributing members of a family or group. Third, children quickly learn to judge themselves and others by the desirability and quantity of toys that they own, often setting off competitive comparisons among peers. These responses potentially reinforce the internalization of class superiority, further undermining children's capacity to relate caringly and justly with others.

As children hanker after more and more expensive toys and clothes, the pressures intensify for families of little or modest means. Even people who have sufficient food and shelter often "feel poor," which affects their psychological functioning (McLoyd & Ceballo, 1998) and can lead to shame and, in some cases, violence (Vorrasi & Gabarino, 2000).

Despite its pervasive influence on children and their families, there is little formal research about the effects of growing up in a society "that constantly tells its citizens that they should not be content with their current condition" (Burnett & Sisson, 1995, p. 27). However, as any parent can attest, even preschool children are sophisticated consumers who know brand names and have honed their skills at pressuring parents to purchase particular products.

Although all children are exposed to these messages and react to the consequent pressures, white children from relatively affluent families may be particularly vulnerable to assuming that they should have unlimited access to resources regardless of how this consumption affects other people or the environment. They are protected from the economic realities that affect low-income people and are likely to live in communities where the environmental impact of consumerism is muted or invisible.

To summarize, as children develop their earliest identities, they observe many facets of the economic system. One disturbing developmental trend is that young children say that the unequal distribution is unfair but, as they get older, they come to accept it and to blame poor people for their poverty. For white children, this view maps onto their sense of racial superiority as they are told that people are wealthy because they have worked hard and deserve their success. Competitive consumerism exacerbates economic and racial advantage and disadvantage because it valorizes wealthy people and, by implication, demeans people who do not have the same resources. As children grow up immersed in consumerism, their identity and self-esteem become more dependent on their purchasing power, which potentially undermines their ability to imagine a more equitable system and their motivation to share resources.

Reflection Questions

1. How do you feel when you see advertisements for products you cannot afford? When you see depictions of opulent life styles on television?
2. How do the children in your program express their interests in consumerism? What do parents say about their children's desire for advertised products?

NURTURING THE ROOTS OF CARING IN YOUNG CHILDREN

As we saw in the previous section, competitive consumerism potentially thrives on and aggravates the messages of racial superiority and economic entitlement that young white children are absorbing. These beliefs, along with ignorance and discomfort about people of color, undermine children's capacity to empathize with members of unfamiliar groups. As Clark (1963) pointed out, "Children who are being taught prejudices are . . . learning to establish their own identity as persons and as members of a group through hatred and rejection of others" (p. 81). Yet children's early capacity to emotionally resonate with the feelings of others, even if they cannot yet accurately assess what others may be thinking, is a potential "handle" for helping children to overcome these barriers and feel connected with unfamiliar people and to understand the effects of discrimination.

The social-emotional dispositions and skills that underlie AB/MC work are an established part of early childhood practice and include "empathizing with others, communicating effectively, initiating and maintaining social interactions with peers, playing cooperatively, and resolving conflicts" (Ramsey, 2004, p. 54). These skills are germane to white children in a way not usually mentioned, because they potentially help them to "unlearn" the unconscious assumptions of racial superiority and economic entitlement that have been woven into their earliest social perceptions. At the same time, however, their sense of entitlement and superiority may make it more difficult for them to gain these skills.

Empathy, the ability to understand and care about how others feel, is essential to forming both interpersonal and intergroup relationships. Human infants appear to be born with an innate ability to resonate with the emotional states of others (for example, reactively crying when they hear other babies cry) (Hoffman, 2000). During the early childhood years, children become more astute readers of others' emotions and begin to see how their own actions affect others and are able to form reciprocal relationships with peers.

As children develop the ability to empathize and understand others' experiences, they are able to communicate more effectively. In many early childhood programs, children learn to express their ideas and feelings both verbally and nonverbally and, most important, to listen to and observe others. However, for many whites acquisition of these skills may be particularly difficult. First, the European American culture, which emphasizes individual achievement and recognition, often predisposes children to feel that they should be center stage and receive all available attention. Second, given the dominance of the English language throughout the world, many English-speaking children assume that English is superior to other languages and that "standard" English is better than other dialects and styles (Delpit & Dowdy, 2002). Learning a range of ways to communicate (different languages and dialects, sign language, nonverbal messages) may counterbalance this pull and enhance children's observation, listening skills, and flexibility.

Peer relationships provide the most compelling context for children to learn how to "read" other people's feelings and needs and communicate with them. As children experience the pleasures and challenges of friendships, they also become motivated to understand and get along with a wider range of people. Children who are absorbing a sense of entitlement and superiority may have difficulty sharing space and materials, resolving conflicts, and connecting with unfamiliar peers. For them, learning how to develop mutual and equitable relationships with a wide range of children is a particular priority.

Growing up in an environment that stresses the European American emphasis on individualism and competition, which often converges with racial privilege, poses another challenge. Excessive competitiveness may disrupt peer interactions and relationships because children do not enjoy constantly being "outdone" by their peers. In contrast, cooperative play promotes children's awareness of others, a desire to connect, and the ability to respond flexibly. To maintain cooperative play, children have to learn how to respond to others' needs, negotiate conflicts, and share power, all of which underlie AB/MC work. Moreover, many studies have shown that cooperative activities and structures are among the most successful strategies for fostering friendships between children from diverse groups (Johnson & Johnson, 2000; Slavin, 1995). Thus, AB/MC classrooms should emphasize cooperative activities to counterbalance competitiveness and to encourage children to form wider, more flexible friendship patterns.

In sum, many years of research document that young children are not "color blind," as so many white adults wish to believe. Rather, they begin to absorb the messages of white superiority and entitlement—the codes of racism—at an early age. Moreover, most white adults do not "see" this process. Indeed, many live out their lives unaware of what is happening to their children and never question their own racist views and racial and economic privilege. There is, however, an alternative. In Chapters 4 and 5, we describe strategies for working with both children and adults to help them develop authentic and caring identities, the first step in the journey toward anti-racist awareness, identity, and action.

FOR FURTHER READING

Clark, K. (1963). The white child and race prejudice. In *Prejudice and your child* (pp. 66–84). Boston: Beacon Press.

Tatum, B. D. (2003). The development of white identity. In *Why are all the Black kids sitting together in the cafeteria? And other conversations about race* (pp. 93–113). New York: Basic Books.

Van Ausdale, D., & Feagin, J. R. (2001). *The first R: How children learn race and racism*. Lanham, MD: Rowman & Littlefield.

CHAPTER 4

Fostering Children's Identities

"As I learn to like all the differences in me, I learn to like the differences in you.
                                        —Bill Martin Jr., *I Am Freedom's Child*

In this chapter we discuss guidelines and specific strategies for implementing Learning Themes 1, 2, and 3. These are the first building blocks for nurturing white children's construction of an individual and group identity that can resist racism. (In Part II of this book we address the last four learning themes).

First, we discuss each of the themes. Then, following the steps of strategic planning, we offer ways to gather information about what your children know and feel related to the themes. Finally, we describe guidelines and possible activities you might use to implement the themes in your classroom. These examples are *not* prescriptive; they may work in some classrooms but not in others. Rather than thinking of them as a set curriculum, use them to generate ideas about what might work in *your* classroom.

LEARNING THEMES

These first three learning themes put the spotlight on white identity. Consistent with basic early childhood theory and practice, we begin with children's sense of self as the foundation stone for learning about others

Theme One: Develop authentic identities based on personal abilities and interests, family history, and culture, rather than on white superiority. As we saw in Chapter 3, white children often develop identities that rest, at least in part, on internalized white racial superiority. This message, which often comes in the guise of whiteness-as-the-norm, is absorbed from countless experiences and images in our society. Thus, white children may not consciously think of themselves as better than others, but simply perceive that they and their way of life are "normal." However, as they are drawn into a culture of individual achievement and competitiveness, a sense of superiority may take hold. Rather than learning to appreciate their own abilities and those of others, they concentrate on outdoing others, often through possessions and recognition.

Moreover, children may become invested in being "special," a self-esteem theme that has been overdone in many early childhood settings (Katz & McClellan, 1998) and that potentially sets children up to feel entitled to unlimited resources and accolades. Therefore, we need to help children construct authentic identities—ones that embrace both their uniqueness and their connections with others.

Theme Two: Know, respect, and value the range of the diversity of physical and social attributes among white people. Overemphasizing the differences between groups and, conversely, ignoring the differences within groups is one way that racism polarizes people. Recognition of and respect for the range of similarities and differences among white people are bridges to an awareness of the commonalities and individuality of people within less familiar groups. Furthermore, as children see how familiar people (such as classmates) vary on many dimensions, they potentially learn to appreciate their own attributes as distinct and empowering but not as better or worse than those of others.

Theme Three: Build the capacity for caring, cooperative, and equitable interactions with others. As discussed in Chapter 3, learning to connect with and care about other human beings rests on core social-emotional dispositions and skills: empathizing with others, communicating effectively, initiating and maintaining social interactions, playing cooperatively, and resolving conflicts (Ramsey, 2004). These skills enable children to experience the pleasures of positive social engagements, to expand their range of relationships and understanding of people, and to deepen their capacity to care for others. In turn, these dispositions provide a potential base for connecting with and caring about unfamiliar people.

LEARNING WHAT YOUR CHILDREN ARE THINKING AND FEELING

To implement activities related to your children's identities, their understanding of similarities and differences, and their capacity to care, you need to know about your children's lives and how they are currently thinking and feeling. Fortunately, many young children express themselves quite freely through play, informal conversation, peer interaction, and responses to teacher-directed activities. Here are suggestions to help you learn more about the children you work with each day.

- *Make time for close and frequent observations for how children are identifying themselves.* Listening closely to children can provide rich data. For example, as children play and talk, they often reveal how they see themselves (as superheroes, mothers, baby kitties, shoppers, bosses) and how they see members of their families (who takes care of the baby, goes to work, cooks dinner, tells others what to do).
- *Keep track of which activities children prefer and which ones they avoid, which skills come easily and which ones they struggle to learn.* This information may help you to support children to develop positive and realistic self-images and to see ways in which they can contribute to the group.
- *Use self-portraits to learn about how your children view themselves and to elicit their ideas and feelings about various aspects of their identities.* Encourage children to make self-portraits using a range of media. While they are drawing, sit with individual children and ask them about their pictures. Most young preschoolers cannot make recognizable pictures, but they can identify particular squiggles as their dog or their belly button. Of particular interest is whether children intentionally select skin-color markers (or paints) and if they make any comments about skin color or other racially related features. The process of drawing or talking and reflecting often reveals which social and physical attributes are most salient to children. For example, some children may choose to portray themselves in the context of family or friends; others may include a favorite activity; some pay a lot of attention to their clothing; others may focus on body parts. Self-portraits also show how children are beginning to incorporate popular images into their identity. For example, around 5 years of age, many girls start portraying themselves as elaborately attired and coiffed princesses.
- *Note children's feelings about their race and ethnicity and other aspects of identity as they play and interact with peers and adults.* Children may indirectly express their feelings though their choices of playmates, toys, and books. Try to see if their preferences and

aversions follow any pattern, and in particular if they accept or reject peers or objects (such as dolls) based on race, gender, ability/disability, family composition, socioeconomic class, interests, or skills, (Boys don't play with dolls," "You can't have two mommies," "Only boys can be firemen," "Only kids with [name-brand] clothes can play here," "You can't play because you can't walk," "I only want to play with the doll with pink skin!").

- *Use photographs and books to generate conversations about culture, class, gender roles, and other differences.* Engage children in discussions about how white people differ in specific ways (occupations, income, rural or urban location, type of home, traditional and nontraditional gender roles, various abilities and disabilities). Ask children to make up stories about these people or to consider which ones might come to their school or move to their neighborhood. Through their stories and discussions, you may learn how children react to people who are similar to and different from them along these dimensions.

- *Listen closely for any sense of superiority and entitlement.* As you watch children and talk with them, listen closely for pervasive desires to own or to be the best. For instance, children may regularly brag about new possessions ("Look at my new shoes!" "My bike is better than yours 'cause it's new!") Or boast about how they can outdo one another ("Your picture is ugly!" "I can run faster than you!") A strong focus on material things and a need to outdo others can undermine the development of healthy, reality-based identities and the motivation to care about other people.

- *Decipher social patterns.* Ask yourself questions to guide your observations. Do particular children seek out a wide range of peers? Do some limit themselves to small groups or stay with a single partner? Which children spend a lot of time alone? Engage in a lot of conflicts? Play leadership roles? These observations can provide crucial information about individuals' social skills and orientations and the group dynamics of your classroom as a whole.

- *Watch to see if and how social class differences influence the peer relationships of your classroom.* Analyze your observations of grouping patterns and playmate choices to see if children divide themselves by social class. If they do, try to identify the factors that seem to be contributing to this segregation (after-school activities, neighborhood gatherings, friendships between parents). Watch for any other ways that children divide themselves—by race, gender, ability, or neighborhood.

- *Observe the overall social tone of your classroom.* Do children express empathy and caring for one another? Are groups generally inclusive or exclusive? How often do children engage in conflicts? How much do they show verbal or physical aggression? Are children generally content and eager to try new things or do they spend a lot of time complaining or angling for the teacher's attention?
- *Listen carefully and be receptive to all that children say so that they will feel comfortable being forthright and will express their true views, not what they think you want to hear.*

After you have begun to develop your knowledge base of children's information and *mis*information, you can begin to design activities (in some cases using the same materials) to enable children to recognize and expand their identities, their roles in the group, and their appreciation of diversity within the group.

STRATEGIES FOR WORKING WITH CHILDREN

Some of the learning experiences we describe below are similar to those activities used to promote young children's self-concept and social-emotional development. However, they do *not* stop with the uniqueness of each child; they include learning experiences that promote children's connection to and respect for the similarities and differences among other whites in their immediate world. The first set of strategies opens up ways to explore the concepts embodied in Learning Themes 1 and 2. We address these two themes together because children learn about themselves in tandem with learning about the other people in their immediate environment. Thus, the same activity can serve both ends. Then we turn to Theme 3, providing strategies that encourage children's development of the dispositions and skills for caring, connection, and cooperation.

Implementing Learning Themes One and Two

In this section, one set of strategies focuses on children learning about their own and their classmates' families. The other focuses on exploring similarities and differences among the children in the group and then expanding this awareness to white people beyond their own families and classmates.

Learning About Our Own and Others' Families

Family is the context in which authentic identity develops. Learning about family backgrounds provides concrete, meaningful ways for children both to learn about themselves and to consider similarities and differences in regard to others.

Provide materials (story books, posters, puzzles, dramatic play props, music) that equally support all the children's families, not just those children whose families reflect dominant culture characteristics. Then, expand your materials to reflect family diversity among whites beyond that in your group. Unfortunately, teaching materials still tend to depict white families, specifically those that reflect the dominant cultural norm (middle or upper class, nuclear heterosexual family). Thus, a large number of white families are made invisible (working class, Jewish, gay or lesbian families; families in which there is someone with a disability). However, you *can* provide images of diversity among whites through careful selection of available materials, supplemented by materials you make with families. (See List of Children's Books in Appendix A and Organizations and Web sites in Appendix B).

Ensure that all of your children's families and daily lives are equally visible throughout the environment and classroom activities. Take photographs of each child and his/her family and post them in your room. Provide materials for children and their families to make posters that portray family members in their daily activities. Ask family members to share stories about their lives throughout the year in the classroom and through audio- and videocassettes. Make every effort to equalize opportunities to participate. Provide materials and be flexible about the timing of visits to accommodate the financial constraints and work schedules of each family.

Monitor your own responses and be sure that you are respectful and responsive to different family cultural styles, incomes, and individual needs. Even though your families may be all white, they are not necessarily the same culturally. For example, in some families, children are allowed to express themselves freely to adult members; in other families, that is considered "talking back" and disrespectful. If you expect your children to speak out in your program, you need to know how families feel about this and help

children learn to express their ideas and feelings in ways that are respectful to their families.

Create admission forms that provide for different family structures. Instead
of offering only the traditional spaces for *mother* and *father*, make spaces
for the names and roles of a wider range of family members, thus accommodating two moms or dads, grandparents as primary caretakers, blended
families, and foster parents.

*Be aware of and respect the religious traditions and rules in each
family.* Carrying out this strategy involves more than celebrating additional
holidays. Different religious rules may also require adaptations in daily
life routines. For example, many Jewish children do not eat leavened products during Passover—even if a classmate brings in leavened cupcakes to
share; Jehovah's Witness families do not celebrate holidays or birthdays
and their children require supportive adaptations in the classroom.

*Explore the range of families within your group and then talk about how
every family does similar "family" things in different ways. Emphasize the many
ways that all families love and take care of their children.* Invite families to
share their favorite bedtime stories, type the stories into a computer file,
and turn the file into a big book to share with your children. Have a teddy
bear or doll that "visits" each child's home for a weekend and returns with
a new entry (a photo and a short description of the weekend, an activity, a
meal, and a sharing time) in the bear's "journal." Consider sending along
a disposable camera each time so the bear can take family photos or a tape
recorder so families can record their entries, which you can transcribe later.
The main idea is to make sure that all families can participate. You may
find that as children hear or read the entries, they will spontaneously notice and talk about similarities and differences in favorite foods, bedtime
rituals, religious traditions, and leisure activities.

*Invite family members to come to school to be interviewed by the chil-
dren about their lives.* Help the children develop the questions they want
to ask their family members. Then use the information from the interviews
in the curriculum activities. Rogovin (1998) found that this activity was very
empowering for the family members.

*Use "Family Homework" to engage families in the curriculum and to ex-
plore the similarities and differences among them.* Eric Hoffman, preschool
director and author, describes how he uses "family homework" assignments throughout the year (personal communication, April 2005):

Once a month, my staff and I sent home a fun, voluntary activity for families to work on together. We would use the results to create bulletin board and table displays, circle time presentations, charts, and books. Since most of the children in my program are from student families (I work at a community college child-care center), they feel very grown up doing what they see their parents doing every night—homework. While the family homework topics have covered all areas of my curriculum, many of the assignments were designed to stimulate discussion about how the children and their families are the same and how they are different. Some examples:

- What are your family's three favorite foods? (we made a recipe book from the responses)
- Bring in something red that represents your family. (We set up a color display table that changed color every week.)
- Draw a family portrait. (We let parents borrow markers and created a bulletin board display.)
- Bring in photos of family members from when they were babies (part of a curriculum on how people take care of babies).
- Find a book in our lending library that your family loves to read, take it home, and do a family "book report" about it. Some families drew pictures; some took dictation from the child; one family created a skit for circle time! (We took a picture of the family holding the book and posted it in the reading area with the book report.)
- Write about a time when someone in the family saw something that was unfair and helped make it fair (the responses made a very popular book).
- Ask adult family members to share: What games did you like to play when you were young? What are your earliest memories of school? Tell us about a mistake you made and how you corrected it. (More books!)

We made a few mistakes ourselves in choosing assignments. When we asked everyone to take pictures of their front doors, it brought up issues of economic competition for several parents, and it angered a family who had been homeless. An assignment about pets left out several children who didn't have any, and was upsetting to a family whose child couldn't have a pet because of his sister's allergies. But these mistakes proved valuable as well, because they stimulated important discussions about family differences and bias among the adults that were concrete and personal.

Be sensitive to the particular needs of white adoptive families in which the children are racially or ethnically different from their parents. While growing up in a white and culturally European American context, the children also need to become bicultural, to learn about their origins, as well as learning to live within the dominant culture. The children (and family members) will also need to learn how to cope with racial prejudice. It is vital that the classroom materials (posters, books) make visible biracial/ethnic families. (Please see useful children's books in Appendix A.)

Explore how the women and men in the children's families play a wide range of roles (some that fit gender stereotypes and others that contradict them). Ask families to take photographs of the various roles they play, with emphasis on those that counter stereotypes (men cook, women fix cars, men are nurses, women drive trucks). Put the photos in a book or a wall chart and discuss them with the children.

Pay attention to economic class as an anti-bias issue among whites. "Identifying social class is confusing in our society. Many people live in mixed class backgrounds. There are no hard lines between the moment when one calls oneself working poor or working class or middle class. But the lived realities are markedly different (Julie Olsen Edwards, personal communication, 2004).

Ensure that children from different income levels experience equal visibility and respect from staff and other children. Among children, differences in family income and situations reveal themselves in many ways. For example, not all children have families who can afford name-brand clothes, so it is important to emphasize how all clothes serve the same purpose and downplay competition about the latest fashions. Children from lower-income homes may need to keep their clothes clean and intact. Providing smocks and having sewing material to mend torn places can meet this need. Some programs install their own washing machines to wash clothes as necessary before children go home. Children from wealthy families may bring nannies to school, and they also should be included as part of the child's daily life experience.

Find ways to create equitable conditions for children from families with limited resources. Some children live in families without health insurance or easy access to reliable health care, and the adults may not be able to stay at home with ill children without losing their jobs, so look for programs or community solutions to meet these families' needs. Some families do not have homes, and their children may come to school undernourished and without access to daily baths and clean clothing, so—in addition to immediately intervening in any teasing or rejection by other children—create respectful, private ways for children to get clean, clothed, and fed.

Counter behaviors reflecting societal messages that equate material acquisitions with self-worth. Interrupt bragging about toys and keep show-and-tell about new toys to a minimum (or, preferably, do not include this at all). Similarly, do not allow children to use their material possessions as a way to make and keep friends.

Create ways to recognize national holidays and children's birthdays without playing into societal messages equating material acquisition with reward and family love. Some families can afford to give their children lavish birthdays; others cannot. Consider implementing a policy that ensures equitable celebrations at school (make birthday snacks at school or limit the amount and kind of snacks brought by families) and work with families on alternative ways to observe their children's birthdays at home.

Document and celebrate the many ways that family members work—both inside and outside the home. Help children learn that everybody does important work! Ask families to contribute to a class display about all the work it takes to keep a family together, (laundry, food preparation, cleaning). Ask family members to briefly describe the work they do outside the home and how it helps others and make a book based on what they say. If a family member is unemployed or retired ask about previous work and activities they currently do for others in their extended family or neighborhood. If a family member is incarcerated, ask about his/her work in prison that contributes to people in that environment or in the larger society. Make a group storyboard about how each child's family contributes to our collective well-being.

Exploring Individual Similarities and Differences

This cluster of strategies focuses on children learning about and coming to appreciate similarities and differences in their peer group and then among whites in their larger community. Establishing that differences exist within your own group, and that differences are enjoyable and worthy of respect, lays a vital foundation for learning to understand and respect diversity in the larger society and world.

Engage children in investigating the physical similarities and differences among children in your classroom or center. Make a collage or graph of everyone's eyes. Then count up the sum of each color. Make a mural of everyone's faces using photographs and then list ways children are the same and different.

Document how children vary in their physical abilities. Talk about and make a book about the children's range of abilities (Susie is fast runner; Josh is very good with scissors; Matt can play ball using his wheelchair; Linda can swing very high).

If children in your group have disabilities that hamper physical performance, engage the group in learning what the children need to fully participate in the program. For example, if a child uses sign language, then teach everyone words and phrases in daily use. Ensure that children recognize all the abilities of a child with a disability and find ways to make daily management activities (such as getting snacks ready) inclusive. Throughout all these activities, stress that abilities and disabilities are on a continuum and that everyone has things they can and cannot do physically.

Demystify the tools used by children with disabilities by explaining how each tool is used. And, if appropriate, rent equipment for children to try. If there are no children with identified disabilities in your program, then use books and classroom visitors to open up children's questions, counter their misinformation and fears, build their knowledge about the strengths of children with disabilities, and teach them respectful ways to interact.

Encourage children to learn about how they have similarities and differences in preferences and interests. Make a book together that illustrates children's preferences (Mary and Peter like spaghetti, but Mary likes hamburgers, and Peter likes chicken; both enjoy chase games, but Peter likes the swings and Mary likes the trikes). Suggest that older children "interview" one another about their preferences and draw pictures to show the answers. Help the group graph the similarities and differences.

Encourage children to see that similarities and differences can coexist and that people can connect with one another even if they are different in some ways. Ask children to list five ways that they are the same as their closest friend and five ways that they are different. Note and address tensions or discomfort that emerge when differences come up among the children (for example, when a child laughs at or makes a negative comment about another child).

Be alert for instances of exclusionary play (*both obvious and subtle rejections*). Help children explore the source of their discomfort and see beyond their initial reactions to new ways of connecting with classmates.

Explore and support the range and variety of gender roles in the classroom. Make a chart of all the different activities the girls like to do and those the boys like to do and note how similarities and differences exist both within each gender and between genders.

Support children in developing all aspects of their personalities and in expressing the range of human feelings (girls can show their anger directly; boys can express feelings of sadness). Help children learn how they and their peers express common emotions (pain sadness, anger, joy, fear) in different and similar ways.

Explore diversity among white people in the larger community. After laying a strong foundation about valuing differences and exploring the similarities and differences among the children and the families in your group, it is time to introduce additional areas of diversity among white people. The methods for doing this are like those for introducing any form of diversity that is not present in your class. Books, visitors, posters, and stories expand children's awareness of the great range of diversity among white people. As you explore other aspects of diversity, always make connections between your children and people with whom the children are not familiar. Remember, one of your goals is to build their awareness, empathy, and comfort with people beyond their immediate environment. It is not necessary to cover every dimension of diversity that exists among white people. In fact, it is more effective to explore specific aspects in depth.

Implementing Learning Theme Three

This set of strategies focuses on how individuals can develop authentic identities that balance their self-knowledge and specific interests with their connections to others. Learning these dispositions and skills within their own group then becomes the bridge to developing caring and equitable relationships with people beyond their immediate environment.

*Encourage children to appreciate their specific skills and interests and rec-
ognize how these skills help them connect with others.* Invite children to talk
about the many activities that they do with family members and friends,
especially ones that show caring and love ("I play games with my sister," "I
help my dad wash the car," "When I make silly faces, my baby sister stops
crying," "I play ball with my friends").

*Make a book together about the many ways each child plays with and
helps classmates and teachers* ("I play in the pretend place with lots of
friends," "I like to play with the blocks with Nina and Tommy," "Josh and
I are putting out snack together"). Keep this book and others created by
children and families in your book areas, so that children can browse
through them whenever they like.

Avoid emphasizing the message that individual children are "special." Instead, help children to see that they are *unique* (this does not carry the same
tone of entitlement as *special*) and that everyone is competent in his/her
own way.

*Emphasize the ways in which each person expresses caring for others and
contributes to the group.* Nurture children's sense of competency based on
the many ways they contribute to the group (helping one another get
dressed for outside, cooperatively moving tables or large pieces of equipment, helping one another solve conflicts).

Provide regular opportunities for children to practice cooperating. Many
typically individual activities that are a daily part of early childhood programs also can be turned into cooperative small-group activities, (group art
and construction projects, classroom "maintenance" activities). Provide a
balance of individual and cooperative ways to engage in ongoing activities.

*Encourage children to expand their friendships to include the range of di-
versity within your group.* Involve children in cooperative activities with the
children with whom they rarely play, to help them see beyond their initial
likes and dislikes.

Change typically competitive games into cooperative games. For instance,
try cooperative tag, where each tagged child joins hands with "it." Very
soon children will be able to run as a group and learn to adjust their pace
and direction to the other runners. (For activity ideas, see Hill, 2001;
Kirchner, 2000; Orlick, 1978, 1982.)

Address the hyperindividualism and sex stereotypes of superhero play in ways that help children value their real power and the value of cooperation to enhance what they can do. Hoffman (2004) advocates community activities that encourage children to connect with others. For example, children and their families might plant flowers for a person who loves flowers but is physically unable to plant them. Alternatively, they might clean up an elderly neighborhood's yard or a local park.

Pay attention to and address behaviors that reflect the hierarchies of power in our society and help children learn alternative responses as you nurture children's interpersonal skills. Children who are used to having their own room and supply of toys may need to "unlearn" their expectations of having absolute control over materials. Children who have absorbed expectations of entitlement because of gender or class may expect to be the leader and dominate the group. They should be encouraged to listen and follow their peers at least some of the time. Conversely, a child who gives in whenever a conflict occurs can be encouraged to identify his/her needs before engaging in negotiation with a classmate. A child who is skillful at getting his/her own way may need to focus on empathizing with rather than taking advantage of others.

Develop strategies that enable your whole class to become comfortable with a range of verbal and nonverbal communication styles and support children who are reluctant to speak or have trouble entering conversations. At group time, create some practices that allow the child who needs more time to get his/her thoughts together or who speaks slowly to have a fair chance to participate. Conversely, create practices to help children who always want to speak to learn how to wait their turn without forgetting what they want to say. Interrupt any teasing directed at children who have trouble communicating (such as unclear speech).

When guiding children through conflict resolution, be alert to family cultural differences in how children learn to handle conflict. When your beliefs and strategies differ from those of a family, discuss these differences with the parents or guardians. Let them know the school's approach to conflict resolution and try to reach an agreement. If necessary, help the child understand that it is fine to use different methods at school and at home. Help children negotiate equitably despite different styles and expectations of entitlement (for example, a boy asserting himself at the expense of a girl).

Nurture children's empathy by encouraging them to recognize the emotional similarities (pain, joy, fear, sadness) among people of diverse backgrounds.

Begin with the children and families in your group and then extend the reach to people beyond the children's immediate environment. When reading books about the experiences of people from a variety of cultural, class, and family backgrounds, ask children to imagine how they would feel if they were in that situation and point out similarities between their responses and those of the characters in the story.

Help children explore a wide range of feelings and interpersonal behaviors and do problem solving about common life experiences and incidents of bias by storytelling with "persona dolls." Persona dolls are large cloth dolls that belong to the teacher; they are not available for children to play with on their own. The teacher first introduces the dolls to the children and gives each one a biography. Then the teacher makes up personal doll stories to introduce, explore, and personalize aspects of diversity among whites that are not present in the group. For instance, you might tell persona doll stories about being rejected because of one's social class, gender, disability, or family composition and engage children in considering how they would feel if that happened to them and what they would like to do. (For detailed information about using persona dolls, see Brown, 2001; Whitney, 1999.)

The activities in this chapter support white children's understanding of how they are the same as and different from others in their immediate world and their awareness of themselves as contributing and caring members of their family and their class. As important as these themes are in children's development, they also lay a necessary foundation for further and critical tasks—developing empathetic and equitable engagement with diversity beyond their immediate world, learning themes that we explore in Part II.

CHAPTER 5

Exploring White Identities with Staff and Families

It felt like I had this big closet to clean out, and I had taken every-thing out and was now trying to decide what stayed, what needed fixing, and what to throw out. It's a big job but it feels great. I know I am going to be more of the person I want to be.

—Student in Racism and Human Development course, in L. Derman-Sparks and C. B. Phillips, *Teaching/Learning Anti-racism: A Developmental Approach*

With patience, persistence, and practice, doing AB/MC work with adults is as rewarding as it is with children. What is more, your work with children on the learning themes of this book will be much more fruitful if there are caring and collaborative relationships among the staff and families. Yet many teachers find it considerably more difficult to raise anti-bias issues with adults than with children. It is true that talking about issues of race and racism with adults can be uncomfortable, especially at first. However, natural bridges do exist. Families want their children to be good people. For many, that in-cludes wanting their children to grow up without prejudice, although that may mean different things to different families. Early childhood teachers also want to do what is best for children's healthy development, even if they do not yet fully understand the role of race and racism in white children's lives. Keep these larger goals in mind as you share your ideals and negotiate your differences with colleagues and families.

WORKING WITH RESISTANCE TO AB/MC WORK

The AB/MC education you do with your children inevitably affects their families; it is not possible to separate your work with children from your

66

work with the other caregivers in their lives. However, without thought-ful preparation and involvement of families, some of them may dig in and resist. For example, many teachers beginning their anti-bias work decide to modify how holidays are observed. However, this change can easily become an emotional issue for some families and staff. If your program has a tradition of a big, well-attended Christmas party, do not unilaterally replace it with an alternative celebration. First, engage staff and families in examining the reality that Christmas is not a part of everyone's religious beliefs and traditions. These discussions will hopefully lead others to see this issue more sensitively and be willing to make the December holiday period more inclusive for all members of the school.

Understanding the sources of resistance from some families or staff members strengthens your ability to be strategic. Mary Pat Martin, an ex-perienced anti-bias educator, explains that:

> Many of the issues come from the way [individuals] have
> been unknowingly socialized about race—taught not to
> notice, ask openly, or discuss issues around racial diversity.
> [Many people] don't see any reason to talk about diversity
> with their children (e.g., "Why raise issues when there aren't
> any?" "Don't make waves."). Most lack knowledge about how
> children develop identity and prejudice, and, therefore, about
> what children's questions and statements mean developmen-
> tally. They do not know how and are not comfortable with
> handling children's questions and responses to racial and
> cultural diversity. Some worry that talking about race and
> racism will lead to the child's feeling guilty about being
> white. They want to keep their children "protected" from
> having to know about prejudice and discrimination at such a
> young age. Finally, even when white families have chosen an
> early childhood program that is diverse, that does not neces-
> sarily mean that they have considered these issues for them-
> selves, their children, and society. (personal communication,
> October 2004)

Another obstacle to openly discussing AB/MC issues is the culture of early childhood education, one that embodies gentleness, nurturance, and cohesiveness and often inhibits conflict. "The need to keep every-one happy or have harmony at any price is not compatible with the strong feelings and knotty issues raised by anti-bias curriculum" (Alvarado et al., 1999, p. 198). Passionate discussions sparked by differing perspec-tives about anti-bias and multicultural issues are inevitable and can produce growth for everyone, if they are entered into in a spirit of shared learning. Experienced teachers agree that it is essential to embrace disagreement, rather than shying or running away from it and to resist being paralyzed by criticism.

It is crucial to be patient and open to hearing and seeking to understand families' and staff members' issues, just as you are asking them to be open to your perspectives. At the same time, don't let either the fear or the actuality of people's resistance undermine your confidence and commitment. You need to forge ahead, yet be open, flexible, and creative in developing strategies. Strike a balance between optimism and realistic expectations. While some people will be interested in and eager to learn about race and racism issues, others will be skeptical or resistant. Above all, have faith that all individuals can grow, although their pathways and timing will vary considerably.

LEARNING ABOUT YOUR OWN IDENTITY

The starting place for working with adults is to deepen awareness of your own history and perspectives in relation to your own identity and feelings about other white people. In particular, try to uncover misconceptions, discomforts, and gaps in your knowledge base that might get in the way of doing effective work. It is essential to engage in ongoing self-reflection, perhaps by keeping a journal or talking with trusted friends and colleagues. Through self-reflection, you will find specific areas in which you want to grow, including understanding your discomfort about some of the beliefs expressed by colleagues and families. Your self-reflection will lead you to the next steps in your own journey as well as strengthen you to work with children and families.

Here are a number of questions to consider. Some may be easier or more meaningful to you; if you find that particular questions make you angry or seem to be irrelevant to your life, stop and think about why you are reacting that way. The questions we tend to avoid or dismiss may be the ones that tap our deepest pain and fears.

- What are the most important aspects of my personal and reference-group identities (race, ethnicity—the countries or the regions in the United States where my ancestors came from—religion, gender, political affiliations, socioeconomic class, sexual orientation, ableness)? How has my core identity changed over my lifetime?

- How central is race in my own identity? How did I learn about race? What are concrete ways that I gain/lose societal benefits by being white or a person of color? (See McIntosh, 1995.)
- What cultural beliefs, values, rules, and traditions did my family hand down to me? How has my heritage shaped my teaching and parenting goals and practices? (If you are having trouble identifying these values, think about an incident in your childhood, perhaps a time you were punished or rewarded, and analyze the values that you were learning in that event. Do the same for a recent incident in your work with children.)
- What are my current social and cultural contexts? What values, rules, and traditions guide my current decisions such as choice of friends/social groups, occupation, and spiritual and political activities?
- In what ways is whiteness "the invisible norm" in my life? My community? My workplace?
- What assumptions and comfort level do I have about white people who are rich? Poor? Athletic? Disabled? Female? Male? Gay? Bisexual? Transgender? Straight? Who speak with an accent or dialect different from mine? Follow a different religion? How do these assumptions and comfort levels influence my interactions with specific individuals?
- How did the family in which I was raised define success? How do I now define success? By promotions and salary increases? Societal recognition? New acquisitions? Family relationships? Working with others? Contributing to the larger community? Being creative? Finding spiritual fulfillment? How have my race, culture, gender, religion, and family background influenced this orientation?
- What roles do competition and cooperation play in my identity? What lessons about them did I learn growing up? How do I react when someone is more or less "successful" than I am?
- How do I react to people who disagree with me about lifestyles? Child-rearing values and priorities? Educational philosophies? Religion?

LEARNING ABOUT YOUR CHILDREN'S FAMILIES

During the first months of the school year, take time to learn about your children's immediate and extended families—their important traditions, roles, and experiences—and how families identify themselves. (A number of the activities described in Chapter 4 will help families provide this information.)

Some family members may consider themselves "just plain Americans" and deny that they have a culture. In fact, they may resent these questions or may feel envious of more "ethnic" families who have retained some aspects of their ancestral culture. You can work with families to help them to see that they all have a complex of identities and values that they are imparting to their children even though it may not reflect a particular national "culture." Ask them to think about the mosaic of rituals (such as Saturday-morning pancakes); roles ("Aunt Martha *always* brings that chocolate cake to *every* family party"); and favorite family stories that get told over and over again (that disastrous vacation trip where everything went wrong) that define their family's culture.

At enrollment time, include questions to help you learn about each family's composition and parenting strategies, which reflect their cultural values and beliefs. Examples of such questions include "Who lives in your household?" "Who else cares for your child?" "How can we validate and support your family's lifestyle here at the center?" "How do you handle sharing, messy play, gender roles?" "What are your child's responsibilities at home?" (York, 2003, pp. 112–113, see York, 2003, for the complete "Enrollment Form Questions").

Another element to examine is the relative status of families in the school and the community and how that affects your relationship with the families and their relationship with one another. Even within racially homogeneous programs, hierarchies and divisions exist. They usually reflect differences in social class and occupations, which, in turn, influence access to resources, child-rearing expectations, and leisure activities. Thus, some parents who are "professionals" (doctors, lawyers, executives) may have the benefits of more money and greater prestige in the community. Their children in turn may have more "advantages" such as sports activities, art, dance and gymnastics classes, and expensive family trips. Other families may not be able to afford these luxuries or may not view them as priorities.

Sometimes teachers inadvertently focus more on the children of high-status families because their parents may be more outspoken than others and pressure teachers to devote more time and resources to their children. As a result a teacher may unintentionally perpetuate the advantages of these children and shortchange the children from lower-income families. This inequity may be exacerbated by divisions and power differentials among the families. More affluent families may dominate discussion groups and silence others. Moreover, they may organize their children's social lives around costly extracurricular activities or clubs (such as an expensive swim club or ballet class) that results in the exclusion of lower-income children.

Gathering some basic demographic information about the communities in which your families live will also add to your understanding of the context in which they function. Through town and school documents you can learn about community indicators, such as range and average of household incomes, levels of unemployment, percentage of people under the poverty line and on welfare, and the percentages of different racial and ethnic groups. By talking to people; visiting the homes of the children in your class; and reading local newspapers, attending community performances, celebrations, and meetings, you can also learn about local culture(s), concerns, and prevailing racially related images and assumptions.

LAYING THE FOUNDATION FOR WORKING WITH FAMILIES

Before you initiate work with families on the learning themes, certain prerequisite activities should be in progress. These create the supportive relationships among staff and with families that allow for discussions about the potentially sensitive topics raised by the learning themes.

Encourage and facilitate ongoing conversations among staff so they learn about one another's views and experiences on the issues related to the learning themes. Staff members can explore their own identities and attitudes related to race and culture in small-group conversations based on the self-reflection questions that we presented earlier in this chapter. These dialogues will also help staff learn about one another's views and open up opportunities to build community among the staff.

A second strategy is to share information you are gathering about your children's ideas about race and their white identities (see Chapters 3 and 4) and encourage your colleagues to observe their children. This topic connects staff members based on their common interest in children's development and creates the possibility for sharing ideas about implementing AB/MC curriculum. The topics you choose will depend on staff interests and emergent issues at the center.

As you have these conversations, you will learn which of your colleagues and administrators may become or already are allies or partners in your work and can begin to build these relationships. You may also identify colleagues who do not wish to be involved. In these cases, respectfully agree to disagree, and create a mechanism to ensure that these differences do not blossom into insidious or overt conflicts (for example, agree to work on other projects together).

Build and strengthen mutually respectful communication and partnerships between staff and families, so that all feel welcomed, honored, and connected with the school's teachers and administrators. To create caring connections with families, teachers can use a combination of strategies.

- First, stay in touch, through a variety of means, including informal conversations before and after school, phone calls, and (if computers are available) e-mail.
- Plan and follow through with more formal contacts such as teacher-family conferences, home visits, and large- and small-group meetings.
- Keep parents up to date with a classroom newsletter that goes home once every 2–3 weeks and describes ongoing AB/MC activities; include examples of children's comments and questions.
- Invite parents to participate in the classroom by collaborating on "family homework projects" (as described in Chapter 4) and school celebrations and joining advisory committees that meet regularly with the teachers.
- Hold ongoing discussion groups and workshops about a range of child development and learning topics, potluck dinners, and work days or weekends to deepen and expand the relationships among families and between staff and families. One teacher invited families and staff to read an article and then write their reactions on a sheet of easel paper placed on a wall near the door. (For more suggestions, see Cadwell, 2003; and Ramsey, 2004.)

Encourage families' and teachers' to learn about one another. If you jump in with difficult questions, participants may feel anxious and resistant. So spend the first few meetings building comfortable and safe relationships among teachers and family members. The following strategies can be adapted for your particular group:

- You might start your first meeting by asking participants to interview one another and then introduce their partners to the group. For example, divide participants into pairs and ask each pair to identify three ways they are similar and three ways they are different and then to introduce one another to the larger group.
- Another opening activity is to ask family members to "introduce" their children to the other participants (by, for example, talking about which aspects of their children they find most/

least enjoyable). Such introductions often open up further sharing as family members hear that others experience similar joys and concerns.

- You can then introduce a Conocimiento display, an activity that came out of the La Raza community-organizing movement. Make a large grid on butcher paper, with columns for various questions (how many children are in your family? where were you born?) and a row for each family member. During the early part of the year, ask families to fill out these grids, which family members, children, and teachers can use to see similarities and differences and to learn more about one another.

- Another introductory activity is to have parents write down values they want to pass on to their children, what they envision their child will be like at age 25, and what they hope that their children will learn from the program. These might be recorded on ribbons that hang from the door of the classroom or added to the Conocimiento display. These comments provide a way for teachers and family members to see the range of philosophies and goals among the families in their classroom.

FACILITATING TIPS

We have found facilitating techniques to be helpful in creating safe and open spaces for AB/MC discussions. If you are relatively new at this work or if you anticipate that the discussions will be difficult (tensions among individuals and groups, the likelihood that some participants will dominate and silence others), you might want to bring in trained facilitators, at least at the beginning. In addition to their expertise at this work, they also have the advantage of coming in without any emotional "baggage" about the program or its history, or about any individuals.

Regardless of whether or not you bring in an outside facilitator for larger meetings, knowing how to facilitate conversations, large or small, will stand you in good stead. If you find yourself doing a lot of facilitating, we encourage you to get some training so that you can develop your skills and learn how to calmly handle difficult conversations (it is not easy!). Also, in many cases, you might want to cofacilitate with either colleagues or family members so that you have more support and insights as you navigate these discussions. As you read the following guidelines and strategies for facilitating discussions, think about which tasks you could do now and which ones seem more challenging to you. (For more ideas, see Jacobson, 2003.)

Create a safe environment. Set and enforce a few basic ground rules for everyone:

- Be respectful while listening to one another's stories. Ask questions for clarification, but do not ask questions that express doubt concerning people's experiences or feelings.
- Maintain confidentiality. No speaking about what others have said outside the meeting.
- Give equal time to everyone who wants to speak. Assure people that you will hold everyone to the ground rules. Telling your own story first creates safety for others to speak and models that it is OK to talk about topics that people may not have talked about before. However, do not confuse safety with always being comfortable.

Keep the discussion both focused and open by using the following strategies: choose specific questions as catalysts for opening up issues and inviting participants to tell their stories; support each person's opportunity to tell her/his story or make her/his argument; ensure respectful listening; pay attention to themes that emerge from the composite of individual storytelling; and summarize key themes and show how they relate to the learning themes

Use a variety of discussion formats, such as dyads, triads, groups of four or five, and whole groups. Smaller formats give everyone an opportunity to tell his/her stories. Moreover, some participants will only talk when there is a small audience, so always have at least some discussions in dyads or small groups. People can then come back together to share insights from their conversations.

Support the range of speaking styles and ensure a fair division of speaking time. Some people will take more time to share details about themselves. Others need more "wait" time; so be sure that people who jump in faster do not take more than their fair share of time. To ensure that everyone has a voice in the meeting, use methods such as agreeing on how time will be divided for each person's story, using an egg timer for each person, or adapting the Native American strategy of passing a talking stick (only the person holding the stick may talk).

Pay attention to power dynamics that reflect those in the larger society. Notice and, when necessary, interrupt patterns such as men talking more than women, or people from higher-income families taking more than their fair share of time. You may want to make a ground rule that a person may not talk a second time until everyone has had a first turn.

Stay open to staff and family members who choose not to participate in anti-bias discussions. While you hope that everyone will want to participate in your anti-bias program, some may choose not to. It is sometimes useful to talk one on one with them to find out their reasons and to explain your purposes in doing the work. These conversations may be enough to draw them in to the process. However, you will not win over everyone. Respect their decisions and try not to get discouraged by or overly focused on those who resist.

Recognize and honor different paths in the overall journey. Growth does not usually happen in a simple straight ascending line. People might change in some ways but not in others; they may engage in some of the learning themes but resist others.

Remember that all adults, including you, are always in process. Keep your expectations open and have faith that people can learn and change.

Hasten slowly. While the work and need for change is urgent, people need time to grow. While always remaining aware of the need for persistent effort, allow for individuals' differing paces and rhythms. Remember that you can plant the seeds, but you cannot force the harvest. Celebrate small victories!

STRATEGIES FOR IMPLEMENTING LEARNING THEMES

In the following section we focus on how to open up productive conversations with families related to the first three learning themes. You can involve people in classroom activities, facilitate discussions about implementing the learning themes at home and in the classroom, and encourage people to examine their own racial identities and related attitudes. As with the children's activities, our suggestions are not prescriptive, but we hope that they give you ideas about how you might proceed.

Every group of families and teachers is unique, and decisions about where to take the discussions and experiences should be made in light of the group's composition, interests, preferred communication and learning styles, and experience with the topics of the first three learning themes.

Once you open up the conversation, issues will emerge that are most pertinent to the participants and that can then become topics for further exploration. Since it is likely that you will be able to do only a portion of the suggested activities, set priorities and be realistic.

Before turning to specific strategies, we want to first discuss the issue of *finding time*, which is frequently a major staff concern in regard to working with families.

Finding Time

You might be saying to yourself, "All this sounds great but how do we find the time to have all these discussions?" Indeed, one of the main impediments to having in-depth discussions among staff members or between staff and family members is the lack of time. Teachers, who often have their own children at home, are reluctant to spend more (unpaid!) hours at the school. Family members who are working full time as well as raising children may feel as though they are barely getting through each day and therefore cannot add a single thing to their schedule. Moreover, availability often reflects economic inequities. Family members who do not have to work or have jobs with flexible hours are able to participate more than individuals who are managing long work hours or lengthy commutes. Lower-income families may be also hampered by lack of transportation and child care and not able to attend meetings unless these needs are addressed.

Although family pressures vary, the challenges of finding time to meet are real and require flexible and creative thinking. First, make meeting times as convenient as possible. For example, instead of trying to get everyone back to school for an evening meeting, provide child care and food and have a meeting when parents come to pick up their children. One way of accommodating people with time and transportation constraints is to have a "menu" of small group meetings on a range of issues that meet at different times and in different locations. You might experiment with early-morning or lunch meetings to see if those times work for families that cannot come later in the afternoon or evening. E-mail discussion groups are becoming more common and may be another way for staff and family members to participate without having to leave their homes. Earning credit at a local community college or university for participating in discussion groups might be an additional incentive for some family members and teachers.

Time will always be an issue. Nevertheless, if you plan discussions around topics that are particularly important to the people with whom you work, they will be more likely to make these discussions a priority. It is also helpful to remember that reaching every family on every issue is an unrealistic measure of success. Rather, keep your sights on finding at least one issue that, during the school year, engages each family in your program. Finally, the time issue, however real, can also be used as an excuse for teachers who are uncomfortable about addressing AB/MC topics with families or staff. If you find yourself delaying or avoiding these discussions, take time to talk with supportive colleagues or friends about the sources of your anxieties and find ways to overcome them.

Implementing Learning Theme One

Activities related to this learning theme focus on family members better understanding their own racial and cultural identity and expanding their ability to support their children's authentic identity development.

Involve family members in the activities you do with children. Many of the strategies described in Chapter 4 require participation from families—either directly in the classroom, or indirectly by providing information. For example, family members can talk with the children about various aspects of their life, such as their jobs and family holiday traditions, and engage the children in specific hobbies, for instance, gardening, carpentry, ceramics, or quilting (For ideas on how to build curriculum around family interviews, see Rogovin, 1998.) They can introduce music and art activities and lend work clothes, tools, and props to the classroom. Family members can also help you create books and audiotapes about themselves and about favorite family stories. Keep families informed about the children's learning experiences through newsletters, through photographic posters of the children engaged in specific activities, and by relating interesting comments from their children orally or in writing.

Facilitate discussions on what families want to teach their child about their ethnic heritage and cultural and spiritual values and ways to do so. Help people understand that culture is not just about coming from a particular ethnic group or carrying on intact traditions from the past, but also about how people live their daily, spiritual lives now. Invite family members to tell one another about the cultural values, beliefs, and traditions that are most important to them. In addition, ask them to consider how they teach their cultural values and traditions to their children—both directly and indirectly. At first, it may be hard for people to name specific strategies, because they do them unconsciously, so try relating a few stories about strategies you use in your home or that you experienced as a child. (For more suggestions, see Carter & Curtis, 1997, and York, 2003.)

Hold discussions about how families can support other aspects of their children's identity development, such as gender, social class, abilities, and family configuration. Since talking about aspects of identity other than race may be easier for many families, it might be helpful to start with one of these areas, (such as gender) and then move on to racial identity at another meeting. If families are interested in exploring several aspects of identity, this topic can continue for several meetings. One way to open up the conversation is to invite family members to talk about the messages they got about these aspects of identity when they were growing up and which messages they wish to keep or change. Encourage them to describe their efforts to make their children feel good about their various identities.

Facilitate discussion about supporting children's positive racial identity development. Since racial identity is not commonly discussed among most whites, (ironically, it is usually only an overt subject among people who hold white-supremacist beliefs), initiating conversations about it will be challenging. First, clarify the distinctions between racial, ethnic, and cultural identities up front. Racial identity is based on the political and social construct of race (see Chapter 2). Ethnic identity comes from ancestral history and countries of origin. Cultural identity reflects evolving values, beliefs, and rules that people learn as they grow up and may change as they enter adulthood. Use material from Chapter 3 and your observations to provide information about how young children begin to construct their white identity and to provide a context for understanding the children's experiences and ideas. Invite family members to share their ideas about how they would like their children to think about themselves as whites and ways they might convey this message.

Encourage family members to examine their own racial and cultural identities and socialization. This topic can be introduced either before or after discussion about what they want for their child. Sometimes it is easier to get into a topic by first focusing on children. However, if family members are willing to first engage in self-reflection, their insights will enable them to be more effective with their children. Select a relevant self-reflection question from the list previously described in this chapter and organize people in dyads or triads to tell their stories. Encourage them to explore how their racial identities and ethnic/cultural roots relate to their current way of life. They can also consider the impact of the history of "whiteness" on their ethnic/cultural heritage as discussed in Chapter 2 (for example, if their ancestors were originally part of the dominant culture or if members had to abandon their culture in order to be successful).

Implementing Learning Theme Two

As with your work with children, learning about similarities and differences among families will happen naturally as you implement Learning
Theme 1 activities. After people relate information and stories about themselves, the facilitator can invite them to identify similarities and differences
in the lives and child-rearing practices of members of the group. It is important to ensure that group members do not make judgments about one
another's ways of life. Learning Theme 2 can also be the focus of separate
meetings. For example, ask people to stand in various parts of the room
depending on their responses to a series of questions about their child-rearing
hopes and beliefs ("I teach my children that boys are boys and girls are girls,"
or "I let my children choose how much food they want to eat"). One area of
the room is for those who agree with the statement, a second area for people
who do not agree, and a third for those who are not sure. Then members of
each group explain why they choose their particular responses.

Create a place in the classroom for families to share about themselves. In
one 4-year-old class, families contributed to a wall chart about various aspects of their lives (photos of themselves, their home, and their pets; maga-
zine pictures of favorite activities and their work; and images of their family's
place of origin on a world map). The teachers added new topics periodically.
The chart was put where it could be easily seen by family members and where
they could talk to one another informally about the information they had
posted (Debbie Keith, personal communication, Septemnber 2005).

*Encourage families to expand their children's awareness of diversity among
white people.* Ask families to relate and then reflect on the experiences their
children have had with white people who are different from them because
of class, sexual orientation, abilities/disabilities, religion, ethnic background, or a combination of these. Follow up with questions such as How
do I want my child to approach people who are different from him or her
in some way? What assumptions and comfort level do I want my child to
have about people who are rich? Poor? Athletic? Disabled? Female? Male?
Gay? Straight? Practice a different religion?

*Engage families in exploring children's books that expand their children's
awareness of diversity among white people.* Appendix A contains many
books for implementing this strategy. Invite family members to practice
ways to respond to the questions their children might ask about the people
depicted in these books.

Help family members think about the diversity among white people and explore which differences are more and less difficult for them. For example, someone may be comfortable with gay and lesbian families but resist talking to people who have very conservative political views. Through these conversations individuals can identify the sources of their discomfort and begin to challenge their assumptions ("When I first heard that she did not take her kids to church, I assumed that she was a bad mother, but I have to say that I really agreed with what she said in the parent meeting about kids watching too much television").

Implementing Learning Theme Three

For adults, this theme is about building cooperative relationships within the group and learning to respect and connect with other whites across lines defined by social class, ethnicity, religion, or family configuration.

Engage family members in cooperative improvement projects for your program. These can include building and installing a new piece of equipment, cleaning up the school environment, or working together to create a winter holiday celebration reflecting the range of traditions within the group.

Encourage families to strengthen their children's capacity for and experiences with cooperative interactions as a balance to competitiveness. In conversations, identify the competitive messages children learn from the media and the ways that teachers and family members may be unintentionally promoting children's competitiveness. Brainstorm strategies to make games and activities at home and school more cooperative.

Support family members working on a cooperative project to improve some aspect of life in their community. The environmental projects described under Learning Theme 6 in Chapter 8 are one example. Another project might be working together to get a neighborhood park cleaned up or installing a traffic light to make it safer to cross a busy street near the school or the neighborhood playground. The possibilities are as broad as the diversity among families and neighborhoods.

TAKING THE NEXT STEP: GOING DEEPER INTO THE ISSUE OF WHITE IDENTITY

With staff and family members who are ready to go further in their exploration of their white identity, facilitate a discussion about how each of them has benefited from being white. Kivel (2002) has a useful checklist for this activity, which asks each person to first respond yes or no to statements, such as the following:

- "I lived or live in a city where red-lining prevents people of color getting housing or other loans."
- "I live in or went to a school district where more money is spent on the schools that white children go to than those that children of color attend."
- "I lived or went to [school in] a school district where the text-books and other classroom materials reflected my race as normal [and members of my race] as heroes and builders of the United States, and where there was little mention of the contributions of people of color to our society." (p. 33).

For the complete list of examples of white benefits, also see Kivel, p. 32. You can also make up other statements that are relevant to your particular group. After individually responding to the questions, people can share their answers in small groups and the whole group can then identify the similarities and differences in how they experience white privilege. You may also want to use another list from Kivel (2002, p. 47) that examines the personal costs of racism for whites.

The strategies in this chapter will open up important discussions with staff and families about what it means to be white. These lay a foundation for moving to the learning themes in Part II, which call upon staff and families to consider their relation to the wider world of human diversity and strengthen their capacity for critical thinking and social activism. At the same time, the activities we suggest in this chapter are only one piece of the larger task of educating ourselves to become anti-racist/anti-bias activists. To fully appreciate what it means to intentionally create a more just society, we also need to investigate the dynamics of whiteness in the context of an economic, political, social, and cultural system of racial advantage (Tatum, 1992). In Chapter 9 we suggest ways to initiate discussions about this multifaceted topic with staff and family members who want to take the next steps.

A Tale of Two Centers

EPISODE ONE

To give you a sense of how the ideas we wrote about in Chapters 4 and 5 might come to life in a real early childhood setting, here are stories about how teachers in two different centers, Mother Jones and Louisa May Alcott, developed specific aspects of the first three learning themes.

THE MOTHER JONES CENTER

(Mother Jones became a beloved union organizer when she was in her 50s and a grandmother. She worked with miners in Appalachia and with children working in Southern cotton mills.)

A full-day, state-funded program for low-income families, the center is located in a low-income neighborhood in a community highly segregated by income and by ethnicity and race. The center families are all white and include single parents, student families, and government-assistance families.

Liz and Charlie are the morning teachers. Liz grew up in the neighborhood, went to the local community college, and, eventually, at 32, earned her associate in arts degree in early childhood education. It is a dream come true for her to be hired as a head teacher in the very center her children attended 12 years ago. Charlie is a graduate of the university with plans to become a psychologist someday. He is taking a few years off to work directly with children, before going on to graduate school.

The afternoon teacher, Marina, taught elementary school in her native Mexico. She and her engineer husband came to the United States when he was offered a job with a large company in a nearby city. She is the only person of color on the staff. The three teachers are deeply committed to respecting families and working with children to build their self-respect and self-esteem. They want the children *and* parents to feel safe in the program.

They decided to be explicit about their goals and call the classroom a *caring community* (Learning Theme 3). They made a sign for the door saying, "Welcome to our Caring Community—Everyone Is Respected and Safe Here." The teachers focused on encouraging children to help one another.

Liz filled small plastic bottles with water to freeze for "owie bottles" that children could run and get if another child fell down and got hurt. At snack time the teachers arranged for each child to have the opportunity to serve, and they helped all the others thank the "server who helps us have snack." When quarrels arose, the staff approached them as opportunities to learn how to live together. After putting words to children's feelings and helping them describe what was going on ("Mikey is crying and holding on to the block. Jesse is pulling on the block and shouting, '*Mine!*'"), they would ask questions such as, "How many people are in this problem?" "Whose problem is this"? "What can we do so both of you are safe and OK?"

All the teachers and parents were enthusiastic about these goals but found that they were not as straightforward as they seemed. Charlie found it particularly hard to let go of his own sense of fair play ("She had it first—it's hers") and worked hard to support children to find solutions that were based not on object-ownership but on the children's relationship to one another.

The situation was further complicated by the fact that several of the older 4's and 5's had younger siblings in the program, and when one of the younger ones was upset, the older sibling would intervene immediately on the side of a brother or sister. In talking with parents, the teachers came to see that for many of the children, it was the important job of older siblings to keep their younger siblings safe in a truly unsafe neighborhood. Understanding this behavior as a sign of caring and protection helped the staff transform their interventions into thanking the older children for "caring," while also suggesting alternative ways the older children could help their younger siblings.

The teachers started the year with a curriculum on "Who are our families?"—and almost instantly ran into trouble. Here's why: All the parents were asked to bring in snapshots to contribute to a "family collage" that would hang on the wall. They were also asked to attend the morning circle where members of each family would have an opportunity to talk about their home. Only some of the families participated.

Liz, who had been uneasy about this approach from the beginning, realized that many of the families didn't have cameras. She also understood that some of the families might be embarrassed about the places where they lived. Instead of pictures, she suggested that they set up a family altar, a sacred place, where each family could display a few items that represented important aspects of their family. They would make a shelf, high enough that children couldn't get at the items unsupervised, but low enough for children to see. Each family would be personally invited to have a week of display time. This seemed easier for families. People brought in such things as a CD of favorite music, a bowling trophy, a wedding picture, the baby's handmade booties from Grandma, and a framed community college diploma. Two families, however, objected. "Altars," they explained, "are for religious items, sacred items—not for family 'stuff.'" "Besides," said one of the parents, "in my religion we do not show human images on an altar." Listening to this conversation (which took place in the entry hall of the school), another parent added, "We're not religious, and I don't want my child to partake in religious activities."

The staff, determined to honor the families' concerns, but unwilling to give up an idea that seemed to be working, went into a huddle. The shelf would be renamed simply "the family shelf." It was hard for Liz to give up her sense of wanting the space to be unique and sacred, but she agreed. To her delight, the very fact that the materials mattered to families created the "special" quality she was hoping for.

The children loved the shelf, and conversations began about home activities. Children discovered that several of them had parents who loved to go bowling and that others had grandmothers who knit or crocheted. "Everyone has a family—our families are different" became a theme as children learned that some families had one mama and three children; others had a grandma, a grandpa, and two children; and still others had a mama and a daddy and an auntie and two cousins. All are families. All of them take care of their children.

Charlie began a chart with the children about things families did together and was delighted by the conversations that went on about the differences and similarities in the families. He was startled, however, to hear Deirdre reply to the question, What does your mommy do, by saying, "Nothing. My mommy doesn't work." Dierdre's mother was, in fact, at home during the day caring for her new baby. In the evening, Dierdre's aunt came over, and Dierdre's mother took classes at the local college. The comment "My mommy doesn't work" bothered Charlie a lot. He started asking the children what kinds of things their parents did and was surprised to find out that all the caretaking, homemaking, and life management that their parents did was invisible to the children.

Charlie suggested to Liz and Marina that they examine the classroom materials and see what kinds of messages the children were getting about the value of what their parents did, whether it was called *work*. They decided to do an analysis of the books in their classroom library. The families in those books, they discovered, went to private doctors' offices (not clinics), shopped in malls (not at garage sales), traveled in shiny cars (not crowded buses), lived in detached houses with trimmed lawns (not in apartments or aging buildings), lived one family to a home (not with extended families in shared quarters). What, they wondered, were the children learning about who was important enough to be visible and valued? How were the children translating the invisibility of their own family members?

The three teachers decided to create a curriculum to address the many ways in which family members work to support one another and maintain family life. They thought it would be wonderful to have photographs of all the family members working to keep their family functioning. One problem surfaced immediately: where to get cameras so that all families could participate. Luckily, one of the parents worked at a local chain drugstore and was able to get the manager to donate 10 disposable cameras.

The cameras were shared. They went home to parents with the request that families use half the negatives on the roll to take pictures of the day-to-day work of each family member. It was particularly important that there be a picture of the 4-year-old doing something helpful (putting away toys? playing with the baby? cleaning the cat box?). Once the cameras came back, a second set of families was able to take the remainder of the pictures.

Liz, sensitive to the feelings of some of the lowest-income families, reminded everyone that pictures did not need to be taken inside the home, but could include buying groceries, taking the bus to deliver the child to school, or older children playing with younger children at the playground.

When the pictures were developed, the teachers made a series of classroom books called "Everyone Works in My Family". The children loved the books, and the teachers used them to create comparisons of the different ways people contributed to family life. Each child received a badge (made by Marina) saying "Family Hero" and listing a particular contribution that child made to family life (for example: HENRY. Family Hero. Picks up toys and puts them away).

THE LOUISA MAY ALCOTT CENTER

(Louisa May Alcott was the author of several books, including *Little Women* and *Little Men*. She also worked for the abolition of slavery and women's right to vote.)

Brenda and Vera cotaught a class in a private preschool that served middle- and upper-middle-class, predominately white families who lived in an affluent suburb. Almost all of the children lived in two-parent households. The three children whose parents were divorced still spent a lot of time with each of their parents. Vera was from a white middle-class family and married to a local doctor. They had two children, both of whom had finished college. She had both a bachelor's and master's degree in early childhood education and had taught at the school for 25 years. Brenda was from a working-class background and had worked in child care for many years before getting her bachelor's degree in psychology. She was married to a construction worker and had three children, all in high school. She had been teaching at the school for 10 years.

Both teachers were concerned about the competitiveness among the children in their 4-to-5-year-old group. No item was too small or situation too trivial to elicit boasts about having or being the best. The children constantly compared their work—drawings, clay structures, Lego constructions—announcing to the world that theirs was best and disparaging the efforts of others at the activity. School arrival was often derailed when one child would begin to regale the others about the purchase of a new article of clothing, toy, or videogame, setting off a barrage of comparisons and put-downs.

Brenda and Vera felt that the children's preoccupation with being "best" interfered with their learning and peer relationships. The teachers were also uncomfortable with the strong sense of entitlement and superiority that pervaded the children's comments. Although specific individuals were most likely to engage in this competitive talk, all the children had gotten caught up in it to varying degrees.

At a parent meeting and during individual conferences, Brenda and Vera raised these issues with the parents. Many responded that they, too, were concerned and did not understand why the children were so competitive, because they did not encourage that kind of conversation at home. At the same time, the parents also repeatedly asked about whether the curriculum at the school was academically challenging enough and wanted assurances that it would give their children "the edge" to get into a prestigious private school or to excel in the public school. In these conversations the parents enumerated items from long lists of extracurricular activities that the children were doing to better position them for excelling in sports and the arts.

In short, while the parents were not deliberately promoting competition, their expectations that their children be "superstars" were permeating their family lives. The teachers surmised that the children were absorbing these values and expectations and expressing them in their own ways with their peers. A few parents, whose children were at the school on scholarships, talked about how isolated and humiliated they felt because they could not compete with the wealthier families. One mother tearfully described her son's embarrassment about his birthday party, which was modest compared to the lavish affairs thrown by his classmates. As Brenda listened to these stories, she thought about how often she too had felt diminished and angered when families talked about their exotic trips and extravagant purchases. She and her husband had worked very hard to make a good life for themselves and their children, but it seemed paltry compared to the glamorous lives that many of the families had.

Vera and Brenda decided to tackle the competition and entitlement issues by helping children see themselves more realistically and appreciate their own and one another's skills as gifts to the group (Learning Theme 1), by exposing children to ways of life that were not embedded in privilege and entitlement (Learning Theme 2), and by stressing cooperation over individual achievement (Learning Theme 3). They also planned to engage the parents in these explorations and changes.

The teachers started by redesigning many of the activities so these would be collaborative rather than individual projects. For example, easel painting and blocks became cooperative activities. Needless to say, many children balked at these changes and conflicts frequently arose. However, the teachers worked with the children on learning to see one another's perspectives and to communicate more effectively, and over time children became more skilled at working together. They even complimented one another on occasion. In a similar vein, the teachers also adapted several routines. For example, at circle time, instead of having children talk about what they themselves had done that day or over the weekend, the teachers had them interview one another and report what their partners had done. To underscore the message that each person contributed to the whole group, the teachers designed some class projects to which each child could contribute (one being a classroom quilt in which each piece was decorated by a child and then sewn together with the other pieces).

Also to enhance children's knowledge of and appreciation for all of their classmates, the teachers set up a few activities in which the children worked with rotating partners to learn about one another's families and their likes and dislikes, giving the class a concrete way to see how people can be both alike and different. They also sent a stuffed animal ("Kanga") home to each child's family for a few days along with a digital camera and journal. Family members then took pictures and wrote descriptions of things that Kanga did with the family (ate pizza, played with cousins, attended church). When Kanga returned to school after each visit, the teachers would show the pictures and read the journal entries to all the children. Children spontaneously mentioned many similarities and differences that they noticed among the families. To ensure that Kanga's stories did not become a source of competition for the most glamorous, exciting, and expensive outings, the teachers asked families to avoid including stories about activities that required money (such as shopping).

To stretch the children's awareness beyond their immediate lives, Brenda and Vera used books to introduce the children to other ways of life and to show them that not all people lived with the same resources that they did. At this point the teachers used mostly stories of white families so that the children would not immediately assume that difference in income meant difference in race. They also introduced Natalie, a white working-class persona doll whose father had recently lost his job. Through Natalie, Brenda and Vera told the children about the hardships that families face when they have few resources to begin with and then lose their income. To ensure that the children did not simply feel sorry for Natalie and her family, the teachers told stories that showed how Natalie and her family were strong and creative in the face of these challenges. The children listened attentively to the stories and often raised good questions. On occasion they commented on how few resources a particular family had. The teachers used these comments as opportunities to encourage the children to talk about how they felt about their possessions and to think what really made them happy (playing with a friend or playing with a new toy).

Brenda and Vera involved the parents in their curriculum planning by inviting them to see the group projects and encouraging them to offer their ideas to reduce the competition among the children. Many of the parents had agreed with the teachers' initial concerns about the children's competitiveness. However, as the curriculum continued, others began to complain. At a parent meeting later in the year, a few parents dismissed the emphasis on cooperation as "feel-good efforts" and argued that "these kids have got to learn to compete—otherwise they won't get ahead!" Their comments generated a lively discussion among the adults. After about half an hour the parents were beginning to polarize and repeat themselves. Brenda wanted to help participants find some common ground, so she asked the participants to write down their own definitions of a "good life" and then three things that they would like to be remembered for when they died. All of a sudden the room became very quiet; most of the parents looked thoughtful. After they finished writing down their ideas, Brenda had them meet in small groups to compare their responses and then report back to the whole group. Not surprisingly, most of the participants had written about loving their families, caring for others, and contributing to society, *not* about getting promotions or shopping.

As a follow-up to this discussion, the teachers and a few parents organized a number of discussion groups that focused on the pressures that families feel to "get ahead" and raise "perfect children." To create a safe place in which parents could speak honestly, Brenda and Vera told humorous stories about their efforts to be "perfect teachers." They encouraged the parents to look at the stress that their expectations for perfect families and superstar children created for themselves and their children.

We will return to the stories of the Mother Jones and Louisa May Alcott Centers following Chapter 9.

Making Connections and Becoming Activists

Part II (Chapters 6, 7, 8, and 9) focuses on expanding children's connection to the human family and their capacity for critical thinking and activism. In Chapter 6 we sketch a picture of the history of white anti-racism activism. We review in Chapter 7 research on the development of racial attitudes and how children respond to their first experiences with anti-bias education. The following two chapters offer teaching guidelines, strategies, and examples for carrying out Learning Themes 4, 5, 6, and 7 with children (Chapter 8) and with adults (Chapter 9). We end with Episode Two of the "Tale of Two Centers," which illustrates how to use the learning themes of Part II in actual early childhood programs.

CHAPTER 6

A Short History of White Resistance to Racism in the United States

> I joined the "other America." . . . I've got this sense that I'm part of this long movement that's like a chain back into the past and will go on after I'm gone.
>
> —Anne Braden in C. S. Brown, *Refusing Racism: White Allies and the Struggle for Civil Rights*

Being an activist may seem beyond the realities of your life, contrary to your self-image, or in opposition to the beliefs with which you were raised. However, protest and reform, including white resistance to racism, have been powerful themes throughout the history of the United States. Activists have come from all the diverse groups in our country and their work has taken many forms. There may even be members of your extended family who have been activists, even if you do not know about them. Becoming an activist is not a departure, but rather, as Braden says in the preceding quotation, a way to "join" with generations of change-makers in the past, present, and future.

From the time that slavery of Africans was first institutionalized and the ideology of racism developed as a justification, individuals and organizations have critiqued and resisted racial oppression, illustrating the fact that "human beings have a unique ability to reflect on their own circumstances and to create, in association with others, a collective consciousness that can lead to change" (Feagin, 2000, p. 34). Each period of overt struggle by black Americans against racism created a recurring ideological crisis for white Americans (Feagin, 2000), and, at each point, at least some whites took up the challenge of participating in the struggle for freedom and equality.

Unfortunately, few white Americans know about this aspect of their history. In this chapter we hope to whet your appetite to learn about it by highlighting a few themes of this significant story. At the same time, our focus on the role of anti-racist whites must not be misconstrued to imply that whites were the only or the primary participants in movements for social change. History clearly shows that the leaders of the long struggle to eradicate racism's many forms have been African Americans and other people of color.

In his fascinating book *Anti-racism in the U.S.: The first two hundred years*, Aptheker (1993) shows that as early as the mid-17th century both blacks and whites resisted the institution of slavery:

> There is no doubt that those who ruled the South were committed to the creation and preservation of a white supremacist South . . . [but] challenges to it were continuous and serious, and the history of the white South is not of a placidly existing white male supremacist society but rather of a society constantly facing challenge, protest, and dissent, both individual and collective. (p. 24)

Thomas (1996) also provides a compelling history of interracial efforts to overthrow slavery and more recent forms of discrimination. The work of both Aptheker and Thomas are the sources for the following review. As you read through it, think about what (if any) you learned about this history in school.

ANTI-RACISM MOVEMENTS IN THE 17TH AND 18TH CENTURIES

The Quakers and other religious groups have often been in the forefront of social change. In the Germantown Protest of 1688, Quakers issued a call for the unequivocal abolition of slavery. They argued that it violated the Golden Rule, traded human beings who have immortal souls, separated families, encouraged adultery, and was based on thievery. Later, in 1746, John Woolman, a famous Quaker, said, "To consider mankind otherwise than as brethren, to think favours are peculiar to one nation and to exclude others plainly supposes a darkness in understanding" (Aptheker, 1993, p. 77). Foreshadowing the thinking of 20th-century psychologists such as Kenneth Clark, Robert Coles, and Beverly Tatum, Woolman also warned that slavery would be detrimental to the children of slave owners, because they "will be possessed with thoughts too high for them . . . gradually separating them from . . . humility and meekness in which alone lasting happiness can be enjoyed" (Aptheker, 1993, p. 77).

Because slave owners and traders defended their practices on the grounds that Africans were an inferior race and fit only for servitude, a number of white ministers and scholars took up the task of refuting these claims over the course of many decades. Aptheker (1993) describes how they cited many examples of learned Africans in Europe and United States—writers, poets, preachers, and doctors—as proof that Africans had intellectual capabilities equal to those of whites. One ploy was to challenge the person who was arguing that blacks were inferior to debate this issue with one of the well-known black orators of the time. In her speeches Lydia Maria Child frequently asked why, if slave owners believed their own propaganda about inferiority, did they so vehemently forbid any learning for Black people (Aptheker, 1993, p. 139)? The abolitionists pointed out that subjugation, not inherent abilities, had reduced Africans to living lives of drudgery: "We first crush people to the earth and then claim the right of trampling on them forever, because they are prostrate" (Lydia Maria Child, quoted in Aptheker, 1993, p. 134).

In the 18th century, before, during, and after the American Revolution, many white politicians and writers vigorously pointed out the contradictions between the ideals expressed in the Declaration of Independence and the existence of slavery. The preamble of the constitution of the New York Manumission Society, of 1785, drew on both religious and civic rationales for abolishing slavery:

> It is our duty, therefore, both as free Citizens and as Christians, not only to regard, with compassion, the Injustice done to those among us who are held as Slaves, but . . . to enable them to Share, equally with us, in that civil and religious Liberty with which our indulgent Providence has blessed these States, and to which these, our Brethren, are by nature, as much entitled as ourselves (quoted in Aptheker, 1993, p. 92).

Ben Franklin, quoting the Preamble to the Constitution of the United States, which he had helped to write, said, "These blessings ought rightfully to be administered without distinction of color, to all descriptions of people" (Aptheker, 1993, p. 99). At the same time, many of the Founding Fathers embodied the fundamental contradiction between slavery and liberty. For example, Thomas Jefferson condemned slavery as "a perpetual exercise of . . . the most unremitting despotism on one part and degrading submission on the other" (Aptheker, 1993, p. 49), yet he had enslaved Africans on his plantation.

Reflection Questions

1. What surprised you about the information in this section?
2. Why do you think these stories are not included in most high school history texts?

THE ABOLITIONIST MOVEMENT AND CIVIL WAR

During the 19th century, the abolitionist movement gained momentum, and many whites, including William Lloyd Garrison (editor of the abolitionist paper, *The Liberator*) joined black abolitionists such as Frederick Douglass, Theodore S. Wright, and John S. Rock to call for the immediate end of slavery (Aptheker, 1993). The abolitionist movement had two thrusts: one was to end slavery; the other, more controversial, was to racially integrate society. Many people who were anti-slavery, including Abraham Lincoln, were not anti-racist. They envisioned a segregated postslavery society with blacks continuing to do menial work, albeit under more humane conditions. As several black abolitionists pointed out, many white abolitionists abhorred slavery but did not want to live and work with former slaves. Douglass vehemently protested that the white people in the North "say they like the colored man as well as any other, in their proper place, and they assign us that place. . . . They treat us not as men but as dogs" (Aptheker, 1993, p. 141). Many white abolitionists were paternalistic toward freedmen and -women and former slaves and kept the leadership of the abolitionist movement in their own hands. After many years of collaboratively fighting against slavery, Douglass broke with William Lloyd Garrison because the latter refused to support a black-run newspaper (Thomas, 1996).

However, several white abolitionists such as Angelina and Sarah Grimké, Lucretia Mott, Lydia Maria Child, Samuel May, and Charles Olcutt took a more anti-racist stand and believed that society should be racially integrated (Aptheker, 1993). Sarah Grimké argued that it was

> the duty of abolitionists to identify themselves with these oppressed Americans, by sitting with them in places of worship, by appearing with them in our streets, by giving them countenance in steamboats and stages [stage coaches], by visiting them at their homes and encouraging them to visit us, receiving them as we do our white fellow-citizens (Aptheker, 1993, p. 138).

Her sister Angelina strained family relationships and challenged social conventions by having African Americans in her wedding party and among the guests at her marriage ceremony (Thomas, 1996). Many white anti-racists acted on their convictions by living in black communities or openly participating in interracial gatherings, despite criticism from many quarters. In anticipation of a united society, a number of white and black men and women set up and ran schools for black children. Although the racial divide remained the norm during this period, a few institutions were integrated (among them, Oberlin College and some public schools in Ohio).

During the period leading up to the Civil War, slave uprisings became more common, and arrest records indicate that at least some whites participated (Aptheker, 1993). Furthermore, many whites were involved in the Underground Railroad, often at considerable risk. Whites caught participating in these activities were usually punished, but not nearly as harshly as were blacks. Many whites were radicalized by the Fugitive Slave Law, passed in 1850, which required, as William Lyman, a Connecticut farmer, said, "all good citizens to be slave-catchers: good citizens cannot be slave-catchers any more than light can be darkness" (Aptheker, 1993, p. 148). At this time, the questions of ending slavery and extending voting rights to blacks were hotly debated in state legislatures, Congress, and newspapers. Although most of these initiatives failed, the speeches and writings radiate the passion and determination of both black and white advocates.

In some cases, frustration led both black and white abolitionists to advocate violence to end the oppressive system of slavery. One of the most famous of these was a white man, John Brown, who was driven by fervent religious beliefs to claim that slavery was wrong. Throughout his life Brown participated in nonviolent movements such as setting up schools, working with the Underground Railroad, and giving impassioned speeches to end slavery. As his frustration grew, he began to advocate the overthrow of the slaveholding system, coming to the conclusion that only physical fighting would stop slavery (as, in fact, it ultimately did, in the Civil War). After his capture at the uprising at Harpers Ferry (during which his two sons were killed), Brown was tried and executed. From an anti-racism perspective, John Brown is a man to honor, giving his life both figuratively and literally to end the evil of slavery. However, in mainstream history books and school texts, if he is mentioned at all, he is portrayed as a crazy fanatic. So while most white Americans scorn John Brown, people from all over the world and many African Americans visit his last home, a site that is now a state park, in Lake Placid, New York, to pay their respects to him and his sons.

Reflection Questions

1. If you had been living in the United States during the 19th century, what do you think you would have felt/done about slavery?
2. What do you recall learning about John Brown in school? Why do you think that he is usually portrayed as a crazy fanatic?

ANTI-RACISM MOVEMENTS IN THE 20TH CENTURY

Since the Civil War, civil rights and anti-racist activism has continued, sometimes stronger, sometimes weaker, involving more or less interracial cooperation and, at times, facing serious repression. The civil rights movement of the late 1950s through the 1960s is often treated as if it sprang up from nowhere. However, it would not have occurred without the ongoing grassroots community organizing and union-based, faith-based, legal, and educational movements of the preceding decades. Some of these strategies focused on civil rights (that is, achieving basic rights for groups denied them); others focused on the link between ending racism and profoundly changing existing economic and political systems.

The history of 20th-century interracial efforts and organizations that predated the civil rights movement is described by C. S. Brown (2002). In 1909, the National Association for the Advancement of Colored People (NAACP) was founded, with the involvement of whites such as Jane Adams and John Dewey. The National Urban League followed in 1910, and during the 1920s, the Communist Party began to actively participate in anti-racism work. In the 1930s, the Interracial Association of Southern Women for the Prevention of Lynching was formed to eliminate that horrendous hate crime directed at African Americans. During this time, a union-based civil rights movement began to emerge as black workers joined unions affiliated with the Congress of Industrial Organizations (CIO). In contrast to many whites-only labor unions, the CIO had a policy of racial equality.

In the late 1930s, the NAACP initiated a legal strategy to end segregation in the education system, which resulted in the pivotal 1954 Supreme Court *Topeka v. Brown* decision. Many whites supported the ensuing push for desegregation, but others openly and violently resisted it. As C. S. Brown (2002) notes, social class determined which whites were most directly affected by desegregation: "Those of low income did the desegregating, the middle classes did the fleeing, and the affluent were exempt from the start" (p. 21). Voting rights, one of the important objectives of the civil rights movement of the 1950s and 1960s, also saw many whites participating in the work. Indeed, some gave their lives.

Since the 1960s, organized efforts to end racism (as well as other institutionalized forms of prejudice and discrimination) has continued, waxing and waning depending on the political and economic climate. This work is forging ahead on many fronts and includes a range of educational, political, and legal strategies. Some people focus more on individual change; others on transforming the underlying structures of key social, economic, and political institutions; still others on the links between racism and the environmental degradation in poor communities. (See Appendix B for information about current groups engaged in anti-racism work, and Appendix C for information about recent white anti-racist activists.)

Just as it is essential that we learn the story of white participation in civil rights and anti-racism movements, it is vital to understand the recurring problems that plague these efforts. One disturbing pattern is the persistent difficulty many whites have had in accepting leadership from colleagues of color and yielding their power and privilege even within the civil rights and anti-racism movements. Reading between the lines of Aptheker's book (1993), it becomes obvious that many (not all) white abolitionists talked among themselves and did not appear to seek input from or accept the leadership of people of color.

One of the most sustained interracial efforts has been the NAACP (Thomas, 1996). Originally, whites held most of the leadership positions. Over time, however, the leadership shifted to blacks. According to Thomas, some white members, such as Mary Ovington and Joel Spingarn, were dedicated to the organization and willing to play any role that was required; unlike other white donors, they were willing to financially support the NAACP without trying to control it.

Despite their many contributions, the pattern of whites acting out their white privilege also became a disruptive issue in the civil rights movement. As a result, some key African American leaders demanded that whites organize in their own communities, rather than trying to dictate what communities of color should do. Those white activists who took up this challenge forged new analyses and strategies for doing anti-racism work with whites as well as acting as anti-racist allies of people of color. People Against Racism (PAR) is one such group that formed in the late 1960s. Although it was active for a relatively short time, its educational organizing work opened up new conversations about white privilege and racism as a system of unearned advantage for whites.

In 1968, the Kerner Commission, a primarily white entity created by Congress to investigate the causes behind the uprisings in many African American communities around the country in the 1960s, issued a significant report that provided an impetus for anti-racism work, which included educating and organizing for institutional change. For the first time, a governmental body named the existing system of white advantage and institutional racism as the underlying cause for the United States's "moving toward two societies, one black, and one white—separate and unequal" and stated that "white racism is essentially responsible for the explosive mixture which has been accumulating in our cities since the end of WWII" (Feagin, 2000, p. 91). The Kerner Commission's report played a key role in both educating a wider range of whites to the realities of American racism and "legitimizing" the concept of systemic racism.

Starting in the late 1960s, several scholars, whites as well as people of color, published critiques of racism and its role in multiple social institutions (e.g., Knowles & Prewitt, 1969). They also analyzed the inadequacy of "color blindness"—the common individual and institutional response to race in the 1960s—and laid the responsibility for the existence and the elimination of racism squarely at the door of whites (Browser & Hunt, 1981; Terry, 1970; Wellman, 1977).

Reflection Questions

1. How did the information in this section compare with what you know of the work to end racism in the first part of the 20th century?
2. How does this thumbnail sketch of white activism to end racism affect your ideas and feelings about being an American?

CURRENT ANTI-RACISM MOVEMENTS

As we move into the 21st century, the analysis of "whiteness" and white anti-racism development has become an active arena of scholarly work. White authors, among them Joseph Barndt, Joe Feagin, Ruth Frankenberg, Gary Howard, Paul Kivel, Peter McLaren, Paula Rothenberg, Christine Sleeter, and Becky Thompson (to name a few) and authors of color such as Janet Helms, Toni Morrison, Beverley Tatum, and Cornell West (again, only a partial list) provide us with further analysis of how white privilege operates both at the systemic and social-psychological levels.

Academic conferences that focus on the study of "whiteness" now take place regularly. Workshops at the yearly conference of the National Association of Multicultural Education (NAME) regularly explore issues of white racism and anti-racism development. Different local and national groups are attempting to do anti-racism work with whites in new ways that avoid the destructive pattern of white paternalism. A national example is Crossroads Ministry, which works with historically white faith–based institutions; local examples include several white anti-racism groups (some only women) that work closely with local activists of color. White people (along with people of color) in other social justice movements (labor, women's rights, disability rights, gay/lesbian/bisexual/transgender rights) are also working toward the elimination of racism and the creation of equitable, multiracial/multicultural organizations and movements.

Historians of white anti-racists do a great service by bringing to life a part of history that whites can be proud of and feel connected to in their

AB/MC work. Most people when asked to name three anti-racist whites draw a blank (Tatum, 1997). But there were thousands of white people over the years, who—much as others do today—educated themselves, wrote passionate articles and editorials, demonstrated, engaged in civil disobedience (one white abolitionist even briefly kidnapped a young white child to demonstrate how slave parents felt when their children were sold away from them), and, at times, put their lives and livelihoods at risks.

Reading these historical and contemporary accounts provides a balance to the pain and guilt whites often feel when they begin to understand how their racial privilege continues to grievously injure people of color. Knowing that this country has always had brave, outspoken resisters of all backgrounds is also strengthening because it shows us that we are not alone, but rather part of long history of protest.

Further, these stories impart a sense of hope: Although the United States has done many shameful things throughout its history, it has also bred strong moral women and men of all races who have fought against injustice. While their struggles have not yet eliminated racism from the institutions of the United States or from the hearts and minds of its people, their work has outlawed some of the most inhumane expressions of racism. As the work to eradicate racism continues throughout the fabric of our society, educators at all levels have a key role to play.

We end with a poem that captures the message of the history of white anti-racism. It was written by Katie Kissinger, a white anti-racism/anti-bias educator and activist from Oregon.

"Diversity: Noun, Adjective, or Verb?"
Katie Kissinger, June 1992

Hearing the word diversity
Over and over and over
Managing diversity
Diversity hiring
Recruiting diversity

Noun or adjective
It's only a word.
Without action
It's only a symbol.
Without commitment
It's only a sound.
Without strong voices in unison
It's only a phrase without change.

Diversity is the nice word
We use now to cover up the pain
and the gut-wrenching agony,
The words of feelings, histories, stories
We can't stand to hear more about.
Because it means we have to face the
Raw, bare-boned reality that we keep leaving out
The same people
Over and over again—
And the loss we suffer in their absence
is too great to face.

So we don't call it
Racism.
We don't call it
Homophobia.
We don't call it
Pain for us all.
We call it diversity.
We talk about it.
We talk around it.
We talk.

Diversity is an empty word
Unless
We can make it
An Action Verb.

FOR FURTHER READING

Brown, C. S. (2002). *Refusing racism: White allies and the struggle for civil rights*. New York: Teachers College Press.

Curry, C., et al. (2000). *Deep in our hearts: Nine white women in the freedom movement*. Athens: University of Georgia Press.

Tatum, B. D. (1994). Teaching white students about racism: The search for white allies and the restoration of hope. *Teachers College Record, 95*(4), 462–476.

Zinn, H. (1995). *A people's history of the United States: 1492–present* (rev. ed). New York: Perennial/Harper.

CHAPTER 7

How Children Learn About Racism and Anti-racism

> Renee (4, white) [is pulling] Lingmai (3, Asian) and Jocelyn (4.5, white) across the playground in a wagon. . . . [Renee gets tired] and drops the handle of the wagon. . . . Lingmai, eager to continue this game, jumps from the wagon and picks up the handle. As Lingmai begins to pull, Renee admonishes her, "No, No. You can't pull this wagon. Only white Americans can pull this wagon."
>
> —D. Van Ausdale and J. R. Feagin, *The First R: How Children Learn Race and Racism*

> A European American child came home from school and told her mother that she needed her hair done in many small braids. When her mother asked her about the reasons for this urgent need, she replied, "There's only one African American girl in my class. The other kids tease her about her braids. I want braids too, so she won't be the only one."
>
> —T. Whitney, *Kids Like Us: Using Persona Dolls in the Classroom*

These two quotations show that children are aware of race yet react in different ways. Some children readily absorb racial stereotypes and use them to exclude others, as illustrated by the first example. Others are able to see that racially related exclusion is wrong and actively resist it, as seen in the second example. In this chapter we will build on the analysis in Chapter 3 that showed how white children's construction of their racial identity involves racially based ideas about inclusion, exclusion, and entitlement. The following sections focus on the children's racially related ideas and attitudes and how they are expressed verbally and behaviorally. We also will include stories from teachers and families that show how young children can learn to challenge stereotypes and become engaged in actions to remedy specific justice issues in their "worlds." We end with some thoughts about the characteristics that go into becoming an anti-racist activist, gleaned from writings about adult activists.

HOW CHILDREN LEARN ABOUT RACE AND ETHNICITY

Children construct their attitudes about people who are different from them by absorbing socially prevailing beliefs as well as from direct interactions with individual people (Clark, 1963). In fact, many children form definite ideas about racial/ethnic groups in the absence of any direct contact.

By the preschool years, children's comments reveal misinformation that they have learned in their homes, in their communities, and from the media (Katz, 2003; Ramsey, 1987, 1991b; Ramsey & Myers, 1990; Ramsey & Williams, 2003; Tatum, 1997; Van Ausdale & Feagin, 2001). One common example is that children who have never had any direct contact with Native American people adamantly claim that all Indians live in tepees and shoot bows and arrows at people. Another frequent stereotype was expressed by a white 5-year-old at a progressive private school. He insisted that his African American classmate must be the bad guy in a make-believe game, because the bad guys on TV are always black.

Prejudicial stereotyping of people of color is not unique to white children in the United States. A student teacher in the United Kingdom, working with 7- and 8-year-olds in a virtually all-white community, gave the children a selection of Christmas cards that portrayed Jesus, Mary, and Joseph with dark skin. Several of the children rejected the pictures, making comments such as "I dislike the way that the Pakis [an insulting term used for people from East Asia] are taking over everything, even Christmas" (B. Brown, 1998, p. 17).

Many white children begin to express negative biases toward people of color during the preschool years. These views may reflect, in part, their cognitive limitations, which lead them to see everything in polarized ways. Young children tend to focus on differences between groups and cannot see individual variations among members. For example, one kindergarten teacher reported that the white children in her group quickly learned the names of their white classmates but repeatedly confused the two Asian girls.

As children develop their cognitive, emotional, and social skills during middle childhood, prejudice often declines. They shift from emphasizing intergroup differences to recognizing perspectives, similarities, and individuals across different groups (Aboud & Doyle, 1995). However, this increased cognitive capacity to see both similarities and differences does not *automatically* or *necessarily* result in a decrease in prejudiced or discriminatory behaviors. Whether children become more or less racially biased may depend in large part on their racial environment (the amount and type of contact with people from other racial groups, the racial attitudes of the family and community). The commonly noted rise in the use of racial slurs as a tool of rejection and conflict during the elementary school years suggests that, at least in some settings, children are learning to be more, rather than less, biased.

For various reasons, some children are more likely than others to develop and maintain racial stereotypes. In Van Ausdale and Feagin's (2001) observations, a few white children consistently made explicitly negative racial comments about their black peers. One white girl informed a black classmate that she could no longer go to swimming lessons because she would make the water dirty. Another time she told the same child, "You're the same color as rabbit poop. . . . You have to leave [the sandbox]. We don't allow s_____ in the sandbox" (p. 109). In a study examining children's preferences for fictional classmates and neighbors, Lee (2004) found that most of the white kindergarteners showed a small but consistent preference for white children and families. However, a couple of children adamantly refused to even consider being friends or neighbors with people of color.

Differences in the ways that children process and store information may be one reason why some children are so vulnerable to stereotypes and negative reactions. Bigler and Liben (1993) found that white children, ages 4 to 9, who had more rigid classification systems in general formed stronger stereotyped images of African Americans and had greater difficulty remembering counterstereotyped stories than did their white peers with more flexible classification systems. In a later study, children who learned to make multiple and flexible categorizations of both social and nonsocial items improved their recall for counterstereotyped information (Bigler, Jones, & Lobliner, 1997). This study suggests that training children to think more openly and flexibly may be one strategy to help children to be less "driven" by stereotypes.

When teachers hear children's prejudiced comments, they often assume that they are expressing attitudes that they have learned at home. However, efforts to find links between children's and parents' beliefs have not been conclusive (e.g., Aboud & Doyle, 1996b). In part, it is difficult to develop comparable and valid ways to measure both parents' and children's attitudes. Moreover, many adults have become adept at hiding their true feelings from researchers and even from themselves. Thus, parents may be overtly advocating cross-racial respect and acceptance but unconsciously conveying racist attitudes. (for example, espousing the ideal of interracial friendships but having only white friends themselves). In a longitudinal study, Katz (2003) found that parents' subtle—and often unconscious— behaviors while looking at photographs with their children (for instance, *not* mentioning race or spending more time talking about pictures of same-race individuals) were related to their children's level of bias. Children readily notice, absorb, and express their families' unconscious beliefs. Parents, however, are bewildered and shocked when their children show cross-race aversion (refuse to accept an African American Barbie doll; express fear about a person of color).

Teachers too may send double messages. For example, using a "tourist" curriculum to teach about racial and cultural diversity implies that European Americans represent the norm, while "other" races and cultures are exotic and interesting but not part of daily life (Derman-Sparks et al., 1989). Teachers are often dismayed when, after introducing this kind of curriculum, their children make many sweeping and erroneous assumptions ("All Chinese people eat in restaurants"; "Africans live in grass huts and hunt tigers"). Children are astute observers and easily perceive adults' true feelings. As these examples show, children often pay more attention to the unintended messages that adults convey than to the words that adults hope that they hear.

Published autobiographies (e.g., L. Smith, 1962) and anecdotes from white college students (Derman-Sparks & Phillips, 1997; Tatum, 1992, 1997) reveal that parental teachings about race and ethnicity range from direct, bigoted messages to double messages (such as being verbally nonprejudiced, but acting in prejudiced ways), to silence ("shushing" children who ask questions and leaving them alone to deal with complicated issues), to directly teaching and acting on the belief that all people are equal.

Finally, even in families and schools that intentionally teach their children accurate information and challenge prejudiced attitudes, children still absorb stereotypes and misinformation from their larger community (extended family, neighbors, peers, and the media). Indeed, both of us know the power of the larger community influence from seeing its effects on our own children. The experience can be quite mortifying! These incidents also remind us of how it takes a great deal of persistence, patience, and persuasion to counteract the racist messages in the larger society.

In short, white children are exposed to a wide range of attitudes about other groups as they grow up. They absorb concepts and feelings from their families, the community, and the media. Some views may be expressed directly; others may be masked. However, we can assume that children are continually hearing and seeing implicit and explicit messages that whites are superior and deserve their positions of power. How children interpret these messages and the impact they have on their lives varies. Student journals and published autobiographies show that some white children who grow up in bigoted families and communities forge an anti-racist identity and behavior in adulthood (see Kendall, 1996). Given the complexities of socialization, we can only wonder if the reverse is also true.

Reflection Questions

1. What childhood ideas/feelings about people racially or ethnically different from yourself do you remember?
2. What have you heard from young children you know?

CHILDREN'S FRIENDSHIP CHOICES

You might be inclined to say at this point (and you wouldn't be alone), "OK—kids sound as though they are prejudiced, but they really aren't because they play with classmates from other groups." At the same time, children often express racist views while playing with cross-racial friends, seemingly unperturbed by the obvious contradictions. The following dialogue between a 3-year-old black girl (C) and a four-year-old white girl (T) illustrates this paradox:

> C cuddles a black doll and says, "This is my baby." T replies: "I don't like it, it's funny. I like this one (holding a white doll), it's my favorite. I don't like this one (pointing to the black doll). Because you see I like Sarah, and I like white. You're my best friend, though you're brown.'"
> (B. Brown, 1998, p. 16)

We can only wonder, if these comments go unchallenged, about their long-term effect on C's feelings about her value and on T's ideas about her superiority.

Furthermore, when white children play with cross-race peers, the racial power differentials that they are absorbing may influence their play in subtle ways, as seen in an observation of three 4-year-old Australian girls, two black and one white, who were playing house. Their teacher saw this interracial interaction as a positive development. However, when MacNaughton (cited in B. Brown, 1998) more closely observed their play, she noticed the unequal power relationships, which reflected the realities of Australian society.

> The two black children (N & T) made various attempts to be "mum"
> but were always firmly told by S (the white child) that she was "mum"
> and that they were the babies, whom she proceeded to tell what to do
> and when to do it . . . dictating, in a commanding tone of voice, the
> storyline they were to follow. At one point, obeying S's direction to put
> the baby to sleep, T chooses a black doll. S quickly responds, "No, not
> that way, you always play with that one, no the other baby," and points
> to a white doll. (B. Brown, 1998, p. 20)

Children's cross-racial attitudes and behaviors are complex and vary
across racial groups, ages, and situations. However, more than 3 decades of
research show that white children consistently show stronger same-race
preferences and cross-race aversion than do their African American classmates (e.g., Fox & Jordan, 1973; Katz, 2003; Newman, Liss, & Sherman, 1983;
Ramsey & Myers, 1990; Rosenfield & Stephan, 1981; Stabler, Zeig, & Johnson,
1982). Conversely, black children are more accepting of cross-race peers
(Hallinan & Teixeira, 1987; Ramsey & Myers, 1990). Van Ausdale & Feagin
(2001) found that white children often commented on the race of children of
color in a limiting or negative way. In contrast, they observed only a couple
of instances of children of color using race to exclude white classmates.

Thus, drawing from several different research strands, we need to
acknowledge that white children are learning the pervasive power codes
of racism, making them more at risk than their peers of color for developing own-race bias in their friendships. Teachers of white children need to
help these children find ways to connect with individuals from other racial groups, a particularly challenging task in predominately or all-white
communities.

CHILDREN LEARN TO RESIST RACISM AND OTHER INEQUITIES

Despite the strong evidence that young children readily learn stereotypes
and that white children, in particular, are likely to form own-race biases
and preferences, we are beginning to see evidence that young children are
able to learn and act on a prodiversity and projustice approach to life.
Observational data from teachers who use an anti-bias approach provide
a compelling glimpse into how children construct ideas, feelings, and behaviors that lay a foundation for this approach. This qualitative information shows that young children—white and of color—can learn to
empathize and to explore issues of diversity and fairness.

Hoffman (2004) found that eliciting and exploring children's ideas about what is fair and not fair was one way to make "fairness part of their classroom's everyday vocabulary." He goes on to say that "by modeling sympathetic listening skills, teachers can help children listen to each other and develop a more complete and mature definition of justice" (p. 153). Examples of his preschoolers' responses during discussion about "What is fair?" and "What is unfair?" illustrate their budding sense of equity and compassion [pp. 153–154]):

- "Everybody should get to talk (3-year-old)"
- "One person doesn't get to be the boss all the time (4-year-old)"
- "If somebody gets too much. That's not fair (4-year-old)"
- "You have to be sure everybody knows not to be mean (4-year-old)"

Whitney (1999) recounts conversations about anti-bias issues that were introduced through persona dolls. For example, 4- and 5-year-olds heard a story about a persona doll with glasses (Rachel) who was called "bug eyes" by some of the other dolls. When asked how they thought Rachel felt, the children said: "I bet that hurt her feelings," "I'd feel really, really sad," "Yeah, I'd feel like crying." When asked what they could do to support Rachel, the children replied, "I'd tell Rachel I like her glasses," "I'd play with her!" "I'd tell her [the child who was teasing Rachel] she hurt Rachel's feelings," "I'd tell her we all want to be safe in our school and calling names makes us feel not safe." (all quotes are from p. x)

In another persona doll story, one of the white dolls (Brad) tells an African American doll (Ianthe) that "You can't play here. Only white kids are allowed in this fort." After hearing what the children thought about how Ianthe might feel ("hurt," "sad," "furious," "embarrassed"), the teacher asked what Ianthe could do and how she could get help if she wanted it. The children offered several suggestions: "[She could say] don't exclude," "African Americans can [play] too." "How would he like it [being excluded]?" "I'd give her a hug." "Me too. [I would say] 'Don't listen to Brad, he's wrong.'" (Whitney, 1999, pp. 143–144)

Children also are able to apply these principles in their social interactions. A parent told Louise the following anecdote related to him by his son's preschool teacher:

My son [C] was playing with another white classmate. When a Mexican American child tried to join in the play of the two white children, C's friend insisted, "You can't play here. Your skin is too dark." C immediately argued back, "Yes, he can. All kids can play here." His teacher asked C how he knew that. C replied, "My dad tells me civil rights stories."

When Louise asked about these stories, the father explained that he had been a civil rights activist in his college years and turned his experiences into adventurous bedtime stories, which his son asked to hear over and over.

Andrea, a teacher of 3- and 4-year-old children in a predominately white middle-class school, had a similar experience. She was chatting with children and parents at the beginning of the day, when Lauren, Lisa's mother, pulled her aside and told her the following story:

> Last night at dinner, Owen (Lisa's 8-year-old brother) said, "Black people have ugly fat lips." Lisa immediately said, "That is not true! Everyone has their own special face, and no one is 'ugly' and it is mean to say things like that!" At first we [Lauren and her husband] were speechless, both at Owens's comment and at Lisa's response. But once we caught our breath, we said that Lisa was right and asked Owen what he meant and where he had heard it. We tried not to jump on him, but rather to find out what he was thinking and feeling. We then had a good conversation about how people have different faces and that sometimes people make fun of each other because of their differences but that all people deserve respect and a good life. . . . To see Lisa, my little 4-year-old, stand up to her older brother and to speak with more honesty and clarity than most adults are capable of —well, I feel so proud and hopeful—and grateful for the work that you are doing!

In yet another parental anecdote, Louise recalls her young son's evolving awareness about Native Americans:

> Our family was camping and met a Native American family using the neighboring campsite. One evening we shared stories about ourselves. When the father related that they were Chumash Indians, my son blurted out, "No, you are not, where are your feathers?" Needless to say, I was quite embarrassed.
>   When we returned home, I decided to get some books with accurate images and stories about Native Americans and also to ask a colleague of Native American heritage to tell my son

about herself and her family. As I showed my son the materials, I also pointed out information that contradicted common stereotypes. A few months later, my son started to do an alleged "Indian dance," then stopped himself and said, "I wonder if this is really how they dance?" Then, a month later, after going on the carousel in a San Francisco park, he announced, "This merry-go-round is bad," pointing to the decorations with stereotypic images decorating the inner drum. I was both surprised and pleased at how much he had learned.

Reflection Questions

1. Have you heard similar comments from children that indicate their capacity for caring and fairness?
2. Do you remember making similar kinds of comments as a child?

LOOKING FORWARD TO ADULTHOOD

Why do some white people become active anti-racists? What distinguishes them from people who either ignore racism altogether or express anti-racist views but fail to take an active role in subverting racism?

Many antiracists are optimistic, energetic, and creative and have a history of being observant and outspoken, often wading into conflicts and challenging the status quo even as children (C. S. Brown, 2002). They recognize that they are not doomed to repeat the past, but are committed to changing the future. They believe that not acting is no longer a choice for them: It becomes an integral part of their identity and sense of integrity (Derman-Sparks & Phillips, 1997). Moreover, by acting according to their principles, whites find allies and make connections that support them and replace those that they may lose by following an anti-racist path (C. S. Brown, 2002; O'Brien, 2001).

Another common theme that runs through biographies and stories of white anti-racists is moral courage, the ability to see through the delusion of white racial superiority and to align one's identity with moral principle (C. S. Brown, 2002). This code of honor keeps people going in the face of obstacles such as harassment and loss of livelihood. Where people develop this moral courage varies: Some anti-racists have strong ties to religion; others adhere to more secular democratic values. But common to all is the refusal to accept the status quo and to ignore injustice.

Finally, the personal theme of anti-racism work as humanizing and liberating repeatedly appears.

> In untying the knot [of racism and other isms], you're unraveling the
> web of lies that each of us has inevitably experienced [and] that have
> taken their dehumanizing toll. . . . in unraveling even a bit of the whole,
> we feel tremendously excited. We have only to unravel more of it to re-
> claim ourselves more completely. (Early childhood teacher quoted in
> Derman-Sparks & Phillips, 1997, p. 137)

Knowing that children and adults can and do demonstrate empathic
and respectful connections to the human family and the capacity to engage
in anti-racist, social justice activism, we now turn to guidelines and strategies for nurturing these dispositions and skills. In the following two chapters we explore Learning Themes 4, 5, 6, and 7 and suggest a range of
activities for implementing them in early childhood programs.

CHAPTER 8

Fostering Children's Caring and Activism

Fair is when everybody gets everything, but nobody gets everything they want. Unfair is when somebody gets left out.
—Jenna, 5-year-old, quoted in E. Hoffman, *Magic Capes, Amazing Powers: Transforming Superhero Play in the Classroom*

In this chapter we talk about ways to develop white children's positive awareness of people of color and to instill a sense of caring and responsibility toward people who are racially, culturally, and economically different from them. We want to encourage white children to begin to understand that everyone does not live or should live the way that they do, and to see themselves as coequal members of the human family. Since this chapter builds on Chapter 4's learning themes, we strongly urge you to incorporate them into your daily curriculum before moving on to the learning themes of this chapter. As in all AB/MC education, learning about others must rest on a strong sense of individual and group identity.

Some child developmentalists argue that young children are not able to comprehend events and situations they have not directly experienced. Thus, they do not accept that children are constructing ideas about people with whom they do not have direct experience. However, as we saw in Chapters 3 and 7, children readily absorb and express prevailing stereotypes about different racial groups. Moreover, we believe that 4- and 5-year-olds can begin to understand and feel connected to people and circumstances beyond their own immediate world, if teachers carefully tie children's learning about others to meaningful events and experiences. Early childhood teachers have the potential to lay the foundation for the long-term goal of raising children who grow up identifying as members of a global community, committed to creating an equitable and sustainable world.

LEARNING THEMES

The learning themes discussed in this chapter aim to expand children's interests and concerns beyond their immediate world and to help them to see themselves as agents of change.

Theme 4: Understand, appreciate, and respect differences and similarities beyond the immediate family, neighborhood center/classroom, and racial group. As we have previously described, white children in our society learn about people of color from an early age and what they absorb is often incorrect, negative information that lays a foundation for prejudice and discrimination. Teachers need to promote accurate, positive understandings and attitudes about people of color before the misinformation becomes too strongly rooted in white children's minds. Through concrete examples, children can learn to see human differences and similarities as points on a continuum—not as polarized opposites. From this perspective, they can learn to reach out and connect authentically with people as equals, not simply "being nice" to groups that they regard—perhaps unconsciously—as inferior. Also, when children begin to see beyond group differences and recognize that cross-race individuals are like them in many ways, they are more likely to recognize the harm caused by prejudiced behaviors and feel motivated to act in more just ways.

Theme 5: Learn to identify and challenge stereotypes, prejudice, and discriminatory practices in the immediate environment. As the research in Chapter 3 illustrates, many young white children already hold ideas about white superiority and "normalcy" and negative, stereotyped attitudes toward people of color that they have absorbed from images and messages all around them, including from books, television, video games, holiday decorations, greeting cards, and toys. Moreover, children will continue to be exposed to racist ideas for the rest of their lives. However, the experience of early childhood anti-bias educators tells us that by 4 years of age, children can profit from learning opportunities that encourage them to contrast accurate images and information with incorrect and stereotypical ones. They can also learn to recognize and challenge the concrete ways that whiteness is presented as the norm and, in many cases, superior. Because of their cognitive developmental stage and continual exposure to misinformation, it is impossible to eradicate all of their stereotypical ideas. However, we *can* help them develop their capacities to think critically and flexibly.

Theme 6: Commit to the ideal that all people have the right to a secure, healthy, comfortable, and sustainable life and that everyone must equitably share the resources of the earth and collaboratively care for them. Americans currently consume the lion's share of the world's resources. Caught up in the passion for consumption that pervades our society, most adults rarely think about the real costs of their purchases in terms of labor practices (outsourcing jobs overseas; unsafe factories in poor countries), the unequal distribution of resources, or the impact on the environment). Moreover, most parents delight in making their children happy and may not consider the deleterious effects of giving them more and more things that then may become the central hallmark of their children's identities. These consumerist attitudes and behaviors reinforce young children's belief that what they want is theirs by right; as a result, for many children developmental egocentrism grows into a sense of entitlement. This profound sense of privilege, in turn, can undermine children's abilities to care about and connect with others. Clark (1963) many years ago warned of the destructive effect of teaching white children to "pursue the symbols of status and success, [while] they are at the same time being taught to compete with others—and to exclude from the area of meaningful competitions those who are 'obviously inferior'" (p. 73).

Family, social class, cultural contexts, and life experiences affect the degree to which children feel this entitlement. For children in lower-income families, expectations about consumerism are tempered by life realities. For children growing up in racially and economically privileged families, budding beliefs in personal and group entitlement (Coles, 1977) converges with and supports assumptions about racial and class superiority. Families who have strong cultural or religious values about sharing resources, rather than amassing them for personal gain, may impart a counterconsumerist message. However, despite material limitations and parents' efforts to negate consumerist messages, children are constantly tantalized and may reject counterconsumerist realities or messages. Social class may also influence attitudes about the impact of consumerism on the environment. Wealthier people often focus on preserving pristine wilderness areas—a worthy cause—but ignore struggles to overcome environmental degradation in poor communities (waste-processing plants in low-income urban communities; nuclear waste sites on Native American lands) and in other countries. In contrast, working-class whites may resent environmental protections because corporations often cite these regulations as reasons for eliminating or outsourcing jobs.

To connect and care for all the human family, children need to resist pressures to consume and should focus instead on developing a broad sense of responsibility that embraces all beings with whom they cohabit the earth.

Theme 7: Build identities that include anti-bias ideals and possibilities and acquire skills and confidence to work together for social justice in their own classrooms and communities and in the larger society. As children develop more authentic identities and differentiated views of the world, learning to take a stand for fairness for oneself and for others is the next step on their developmental journey. Experience has shown that teachers can effectively engage children as young as 4 years old in activism if the projects emerge from real incidents or issues in their lives; are simple and direct; have a clear, tangible focus; and are geared to the children's experiences rather than to achieving a particular outcome. By participating in these learning opportunities, children learn to act responsibly; consider people's feelings, perspectives, and ideas; and notice how their actions might affect other people (Pelo & Davidson, 2000).

Just like white adults who are struggling to form anti-racist identities, children need role models of courageous white anti-racists. Children love stories of adventure and courage. Learning about the struggles and victories of anti-racists—whites and people of color—is a way of channeling this fascination away from films, television shows, and video games in which strength and courage are measured only by violent actions that often reflect racist and sexist themes. We need to imbue our children with courage and a sense of possibility that rest, not on dreams of individual entitlement, but on the desire to make the world a better place for everyone.

LEARNING WHAT YOUR CHILDREN ARE THINKING AND FEELING

As we stated in Chapter 4, regularly observing, listening to, and informally talking with your children are essential to implementing relevant AB/MC curriculum. Needless to say, each child will have a unique "take" on these issues, and we will never know all that each child thinks and feels about them. However, as you listen and observe, you will get a sense of the range of ideas that children are developing, which will, in turn, help you to design activities that potentially enlarge children's realm of caring and strengthen and deepen their commitment to fairness.

The techniques for learning how children feel about different groups of people are similar to those we suggested in Chapter 4, although specific questions are different.

- *Use photographs and books that depict a wide range of people of color and their daily lives in the United States to elicit children's thoughts and feelings about different groups.* With individual children and with small groups, you might ask questions such as, What do you notice about the person? What might this person do for fun or for work? In addition to seeking children's ideas about different aspects of diversity, note their emotional reactions: Do any children laugh? Ask questions? Seem interested? Scornful? When children see pictures or hear stories about people with more/less money, how do they react? Do they "blame" poor people for their plight or are they more sympathetic and respectful? Do they assume that rich people are better or happier than poor people? Ask children which of the people depicted in the photographs they would like to have join their class or live in their neighborhood. Then explore the reasons behind their selections. Encourage children to make up stories about the people in some of the pictures.

- *Note any comments implying that people of color are deviant or inferior that children make in their play or conversations.* For example, early childhood teachers have reported hearing the following comments: "His skin looks like mud. Yuk!" "Chinese people can't see good 'cause their eyes are kinda shut," "Look! I am sitting 'Indian style,'" "Arabs kill people," and "Vietnamese people talk funny." These comments can become the starting point for planning activities to challenge beliefs that may be precursers to prejudice.

- *Ask children and family members about children's previous contacts with groups other than their own.* What groups are represented in their neighborhood, social groups, place of worship, and workplace? Have families traveled or lived in other cities and regions in the United States or other countries? Were they tourists or did they live as members of the local community? How did their children react to unfamiliar people and situations? These questions can be incorporated into your initial intake interview, as well as your ongoing conversations with families (as described in Chapter 5). How families tell their stories provides a glimpse into their views of people who are different from themselves (such as describing other customs/lifestyles respectfully or disdainfully).

- *Observe how children and family members view possessions.* How often do children come into school reciting a catalog of their new purchases? How much attention do they pay to one another's new clothes? New toys? Do they tease children who wear worn clothing or shoes? Do they use new, "hot" toys to entice or control other children? Do they appear to be highly influenced by television commercials? How do the families feel toward consumerism and social-class differences? Do they talk a lot about possessions? Fancy trips? How competitive or cooperative are they with other families in the program? Do wealthier families ignore families with lower incomes?

- *Observe how children react to the natural environment.* How do children react to the animals and plants in your classroom? Do they take an interest? Think about what other living things need? What do children do when they are outside? Do they express curiosity and concern about plants and animals or do they tend to "conquer" nature (pretend to chop down trees, avoid or destroy bugs when they see them)? Do they notice litter and other local environmental problems?
- *Watch how children react to unfair situations.* Are there frequent situations in which children are unfair or mean to each other? How do others react to these situations? Do children stand up for themselves and others? Do they seem to understand the concept of fairness (not just use it to justify what they want)?

STRATEGIES FOR WORKING WITH CHILDREN

The strategies we suggest in this chapter build on children's previous exploration of similarities and differences among whites and the creating of caring connections within their immediate world (see Chapter 4). The goals are for children to understand how people from *all* groups share commonalities and differences and to construct the attitudes and skills to eventually help build a diverse society free of racism.

Implementing Learning Theme Four

This set of strategies focuses on differences and similarities beyond white children's immediate environment. They are similar to those found in other anti-bias and multicultural curriculum resources (e.g., Derman-Sparks et al., 1989; Ramsey, 2004; Wolpert, 2002; York, 2003). Remember to connect this learning theme to children's understanding of similarities and differences among themselves.

Model inclusive practices. How you set up and use your aesthetic and material environment sets the stage for expanding your children's learning about racial and cultural diversity. If your visual and material environment is filled with diverse images, it immediately tells children and families that this is a priority for you. Therefore, while displaying images of the children in your program is essential, it is equally essential to bring the diversity of people in the United States into children's daily lives. If you have families in your program who are from other countries, then make sure to include images of those countries. However, avoid exotic images of people from places that are completely unfamiliar to children.

For infant and toddler groups, it is particularly important to introduce unfamiliar images slowly, while balancing them with depictions of familiar people and situations, and to limit the amount of images and materials (Janet Gonzlaes-Mena, personal communication, 2004).

Make an inventory of your current educational materials and work on building a collection of materials that accurately depict the diversity within all groups (including whites) in the United States. Include materials that reflect the many ways that people live (urban, rural, suburban; poor, working class, middle class, wealthy; small and large families); how they look (different skin tones, facial features, and body types); what they wear (traditional or contemporary clothing); and what they do (people with a number of abilities and disabilities; women and men in a range of occupations and roles). In particular, be sure that many of the images counteract common stereotypes.

Use these materials regularly in your on-going curriculum, not just at "special" times. For example, choose books with people of color to explore basic early childhood themes such as friends, a new baby in the family, the first day of school, grandparents, birthdays, or holiday celebrations.

Watch to see if children avoid playing with certain materials and try to counteract their avoidance. For example, if children are not playing with the African American or Asian doll, join their dramatic play and make a point of holding and taking care of that doll, emphasizing how much you are enjoying playing with it. Try to incorporate the doll into their play rather than coercing the children to play with it.

Explore the racial and cultural diversity that exists in the children's larger community, always making it concrete and individualized. With preschoolers and kindergarten-age children, focus on the immediate community and city (for instance, taking neighborhood walks). With 6- to 8-year-olds, you can move further afield (state and country), using photographic essays, books, and so on.

Regularly schedule people from different racial and ethnic groups to do a series of specific activities with your children. Ongoing face-to-face contact is probably the best way to break down barriers, recognize similarities, and see differences as enriching rather than frightening or distasteful. Be sure that visitors are introduced as complex real people (with families, specific interests and tastes, particular ways of doing things) not as representatives of a class of people. Hoffman (2004) explains, "When I ask someone to be an 'example' for my curriculum, I don't want the children to think of that person in only one way. . . . I ask the person beforehand for three things he or she would like the children to know about them and focus on those" (p. 166).

Enhance children's sense of connection with others by exploring how people meet similar needs in different ways. Explore the many different ways people manage day-to-day life (carry babies or put them to sleep, live in different types of houses, prepare food).

If you take field trips to visit people in the community, make the outings purposeful. Go to a store to buy materials for the classroom, visit people to learn about their interesting work. Avoid one-time, superficial field trips or visits, because these experiences may only reinforce children's stereotypes about different racial or cultural groups.

Tell persona doll stories that explore differences and similarities beyond children's immediate experiences in meaningful and empathic ways. Make sure the stories authentically reflect real, "ordinary" lives in your community by getting help from colleagues or friends from that group. Always use more than one doll of a particular group and tell stories that are about everyday experiences to illustrate similarities as well as differences between your children and the dolls. Also maintain a balance between positive experiences, such as family visits and celebrations, and challenging ones, such as handling prejudice.

Talk about why people have different skin colors. All the Colors We Are, by Katie Kissinger (1994), is one of several excellent resources for these discussions. Written in English and Spanish, the book includes several suggestions for discussing skin color with preschool children that are based on the author's many years of experience as an early childhood teacher.

Teach children everyday words that people use to carry out shared human activities in languages other than English. Teaching these words (words for family members, expressions of feeling, foods, numbers, colors) in languages other than English helps children experience and explore their connections with others in a concrete form. Use persona dolls to introduce words that are spoken in their "families." Label materials around the room in more than one language. Use different languages when you sing songs or do counting activities.

With 5- to 8-year-olds, begin to connect different ways of meeting similar needs with the environments in which people live. For example, you might create puppet shows or skits to show how someone from another type of community or climate finds your ways to be strange (a rural child wondering how city children manage without land and a creek to play in or a child who comes from a warm climate being surprised by snow).

Implementing Learning Theme Five

The following strategies build on the work you have done creating caring, respectful connections between the children in your program as discussed in Chapters 3 and 4. As you work to counter children's stereotypes and discomforts, be conscious of the reality that every day they are being exposed to misinformation. At times it may feel like a losing battle. Do not get discouraged; expect that it will take a long time and many discussions for children to learn to resist this pull.

Use children's biased remarks as teachable moments. Although children may not understand the full meaning of their biased comments, these can become the basis for more developed prejudice if adults do not respond to them. When you hear such a comment, immediately follow up with exploratory questions to gain a deeper understanding of the child's thoughts and feelings ("What do you mean by that?" "How do you know that?" "Do you think that all the people there do _____? What about moms and dads and kids?"). Use an exploratory, rather than accusatory, tone. Ask questions in ways that let you into the children's thinking, rather than close them down. Then plan both immediate and longer–term experiences, as illustrated by the following example from Eric Hoffman (personal communication, April 2005):

> "Did you hear what those children said?" The parent's question drew my attention to four 4-year-olds sitting at a table, talking and giggling. To me, they looked like they had found a good way to get away from the crowd and relax, but when I focused on their words, I understood the parent's distress. They were repeating a jingle that made fun of Chinese people. The children were clearly unaware that their language was racist. Their interest was in the silly sounds and their feelings of friendship.
> "I hear you saying a rhyme that makes you laugh." They started to repeat the words, but I stopped them. "Do you know what the word *Chinese* means?" They all shook their heads. I explained that it referred to people from a part of the world called

China, and that Chinese people would be insulted by the jingle. They were taken aback—that was not their intention.

"I know one that's not about Chinese," a child said, and he started saying another rhyme that made fun of Asian eyes. I explained that even though the new rhyme didn't mention Chinese people, it was still making fun of people. I started to explain about Asia and China, but I could see that my geography lesson was beyond their comprehension.

"It looks like you're not trying to hurt anybody's feelings. You want to be friends and laugh about silly words. So let's think of some that won't upset anyone." We came up with a great list of ridiculous rhymes that left them rolling on the floor with laughter. I felt good about how I handled the situation, until I heard one of the children say to another, "You shouldn't say Chinese. That's a bad word."

In discussing with my staff how we should respond, I was struck by a dilemma that is common in anti-bias work: How do you help people unlearn racism without hurting those who are the targets of that racism? We wanted to create curriculum that would help the children develop positive feelings about ethnic and national differences. However, we knew that we ran the risk of uncovering more racist ideas. We didn't want the children to censor themselves out of fear they would be punished; it felt important to get those misconceptions out in the open so they could be challenged. On the other hand, allowing children to voice racism, even when it is unintended, can damage children who are members of the targeted group. People of color shouldn't be forced to listen in while white people work out their racism. I find this especially important to keep in mind in groups where there is little ethnic or racial diversity, because it's so easy to dismiss the feelings of the minority when there is no one around to express them.

One way to make sure those feelings are heard is through persona dolls. By introducing a variety of dolls at the beginning of the year, I can bring people to my class who can voice the unfairness of name-calling and discrimination. If I have used the dolls correctly and brought them to life, young children will respond to those voices with compassion and work hard to correct the injustice.

So when my staff and I planned our new curriculum we didn't start with lectures and geography lessons, we started with feelings. One of the dolls talked about her wonderful Vietnamese family and how much she hated being made fun of for her differences. She spoke with great pride and great pain. That opened the door for many discussions about ethnic labels, places in the world, ancestors, and how much it hurts to have someone make fun of the way you look, speak, or act.

Help children recognize stereotypes and incorrect information, and appreciate the harm they can do. When you read stories or show pictures that have stereotypes, encourage the children to identify them and talk about why they are not fair. Wolpert (1999) suggests playing a "Stereotype or Fact" game with older preschoolers and kindergarteners to help them explore the differences between a stereotype and a fact. The teacher makes exaggerated statements that the children know from experience are obviously not true, such as, "All children hate ice cream." Then she asks if the statement is true or false and how the children know. Some of the teacher's statements can also be tested out by the children, as in, "Only boys know how to run." After trying out several similar kinds of statements, the teacher explains that the untrue statements are called *stereotypes*, because they say "all children" or "all boys", and so on, even when it isn't true for everyone. Then, when children make a stereotypical comment about a person/group not in their experience, the teacher can refer to the Stereotype or Fact game as one way to introduce critical thinking about misinformation.

Start exploring stereotypes with statements about gender. Preschool children are very concerned about gender identification, often express gender stereotypes, and exclude peers along these lines. Thus, addressing gender-related assumptions is a good way to begin. Moreover, children can "test" these beliefs against their own experiences. For instance, make a list with the children of the activities boys like and the activities girls like. Then take photographs of play in the classroom and playground and compare the photographs with the list. What do children notice? Should any changes to the list be made? Encourage children to talk about times that they have been teased, rejected, or told that they couldn't play with a particular toy, because of being a girl or a boy. How did they feel when that happened.

Next, work in a similar way with children's ideas about people of color, which you may have documented in your information gathering. Provide images and books that challenge the common stereotypes to which children are exposed in society and help children see and think about the contrast between what they may think and what is real. For example, contrast young children's common belief that all American Indians live in tepees or shoot people with bows and arrows with photographs and books about real contemporary American Indians.

Engage children in critiquing children's books that only include images of whites or that depict inaccurate images of people of color. Ask children to imagine each story with more diverse characters or accurate images ("Could this character be a person with dark skin instead of a white skin?" "Do you think that this book tells the truth/is fair to Vietnamese people?"). Invite children to dictate or write letters to authors about what they like and do not like in their stories and how they could make future stories more inclusive.

Spark children's empathy about the hurt that stereotypes can cause. As we saw in the previous example of Eric Hoffman's use of a teachable moment with a group of preschoolers, persona doll stories are especially helpful for these explorations. A doll of color can talk about being teased or excluded by her white peers because of skin color or being in a classroom where there are no images of people who look like her. As you tell the persona doll story, involve children in exploring the doll's feelings and how it feels to be the target of prejudice or discrimination. Then, ask children to help figure out what they would do to stop the discrimination described in the story. You can do many stories throughout the school year that address many types of prejudice and discrimination.

Promote children's capacity to problem-solve ways to handle incidents of prejudice and discrimination. As with the previous activities in this chapter, begin with incidents in your own classroom or in your children's lives, and then make the bridge to prejudice and discrimination directed against others. Use conflict-resolution strategies to help children resolve incidents that involve being teased or rejected because of an aspect of identity (excluding children on the basis of dress, always assigning a small child the "baby" role in dramatic play, teasing a child who wears glasses). Use these incidents to help children understand the impact of discrimination directed at people not in their immediate environment.

Implementing Learning Theme Six

We now move on to strategies for promoting children's interest in the care of the environment and in sharing resources.

Nurture children's respect, love, and sense of responsibility for the well-being of the natural environment. Involve children in the traditional early childhood education activities of planting and caring for classroom plants and animals as a first step. If possible, take field trips to explore different types of natural environments in your community.

Engage children in taking care of the environment around them. Pick up litter. Start a recycling program. Analyze the trash in your classroom and think of ways to decrease the use of disposable materials.

Help children identify and work on local environmental problems. Invite local environmental activists to tell the children about what they do, and find ways for the children to visit and participate in some of their activities. Find meaningful ways to involve children. Learning about the destruction of distant environments may not be an effective starting point, but cleaning up a favorite park would be.

When engaged in cooking projects or eating new foods, talk about where food comes from. Help children think about what plants and animals need to survive. They can also think about the farmers who plowed the fields and nurtured and harvested the plants. If you are eating a food that is from a different climate, talk about that part of the country or world and what it would be like to live there.

Encourage children to develop a sense of responsibility in regard to people in their community and to think about how to distribute resources equitably. Organize and participate in toy and clothing exchanges for families in the center and immediate neighborhood or food and toy collections for community organizations or food distribution centers. Be sure these efforts are not one-time superficial acts of "charity." Work closely with one organization and, if possible, have children spend time with their clients. If that cannot be arranged, invite a staff member to visit your program and talk about some of the individuals who are receiving the food and clothing. In this way children see people who are poor as individuals who are very much like them in many ways. This perspective may help to inoculate children from absorbing and believing common stereotypes of poor people. To avoid fostering stereotypes about class and race, be careful not to focus on only one racial or ethnic group. (For an excellent example of this kind of action project, see Pelo & Davidson, 2000).

With children 5 to 8 years old, create situations that draw children's attention to economic inequities in the wider community. You can use role-playing activities to raise these issues. For example, in one kindergarten serving middle- and upper-middle-class children, the teachers set up a store in the role-playing area but gave children different amounts of "money" to spend. One of the teachers described the follow-up discussions, in which the children expressed their strong reactions the situation and offered a number of solutions to the make it fairer.

> Kyle, Ashley, and Blake (among others) suggested sharing the food with the group after each shopping trip. . . . Eva, Josiah, and Corey suggested that the group should redistribute the money more evenly. . . . Josiah is adamant on this point saying, "everyone should have two [play dollars]" and later "I want to play the fair and square way." (Lee, 2004, pp. 74)

Discussions of social class grew beyond the store activity. The teachers used photographs and stories that depicted people in different economic circumstances to help children make the connection between their immediate "store" experience and broader equity issues. In a discussion with Corey and Josiah, one of the teachers asked "How do people get money?" to which Corey replied, "At the bank. Some people have zero dollars." When the teacher asked them both about jobs, Josiah said, "My dad has a job so we have money." Later the boys and the teacher decided that they would "work" (tidy the pretend area) to earn their two dollars for shopping (Lee, 2004, pp. 74–75).

These conversations are consistent with previous research findings (e.g., Furnham & Stacey, 1991) that children at 5 and 6 years old are able to understand the concrete ideas of wealth (buying and selling; money) and offer equitable solutions, although they cannot yet understand some of the larger questions (for example, "How do people get money?").

Teach children about environmental activists who work on issues that the children are exploring. Here is an example from the Dandelion School, in Cambridge, Massachusetts, a full-service child-care program that serves a racially and economically diverse population and practices anti-bias education. Expanding on the children's typical preschooler interest in animals, which had led to their making zoos, farms, jungles, and aquariums for their rubber animals, the teachers introduced *The Great Kapok Tree*, by Lynne Cherry (1990). Like most of the book's readers, the children learned about the need to protect the Amazon rain forest and its animals. Unlike most readers, however, they also learned about Chico Mendes, a rubber tapper and environmentalist whose campaign to save the rain forest from exploitation by industrialists and large landowners inspired Cherry to write her book. Similarly, when the children became interested in sharks and other fish, this sparked a wider concern about oceans. The teachers did some research about environmental activism and learned of diver Sylvia Earl's work to protect the oceans. While the children enjoyed playing "deep-sea diver," they also became intrigued by Dr. Earl's work and began asking questions about how they could help to make the water cleaner. (Kathy Roberts, personal communication, June 2005).

Implementing Learning Theme Seven

This final set of strategies is aimed at fostering children's activism skills and their confidence that they can make a difference.

Engage children in democratic social processes by involving them in creating group/classroom structures that are fair to everyone. Include children in deciding on classroom procedures and rules. Obviously, the latitude that we give children in these decisions varies by age. However, children at all ages have ideas about helpful and hurtful interpersonal behaviors and usually eagerly contribute ideas about how to make the classroom "safe" for everyone (for example, no hitting). Children can also begin to discuss how to ensure that everyone has an equal voice in discussions and equitably participates in making classroom decisions. In the process of deciding on procedures and rules, children experience the interdependence of all members of the class and the need to be flexible. They learn to articulate their own needs; listen to the opinions of others; see their own needs and views in a broader perspective; and think about the purpose, fairness, and enforcement of the rules. They also experience on a small scale what it takes for a society to function and what skills are needed to organize democratic communities. (For more details on making decisions about classroom rules and routines, see Ramsey 2004.)

Engage children in activism related to issues that are meaningful and relevant to them. Remember that these activities are not about changing the world from an adult's perspective, but rather about children making their own worlds a little fairer. Use the following steps to design appropriate activism projects:

1. *Listen to and observe what is happening in your early childhood classroom and in the larger community of your program* Be alert to specific unfair situations and practices in the life of the classroom or immediate community that directly affect the children's lives. For example, you might notice that only the boys use the block area or realize that the classroom space needs to be reorganized to accommodate a child who uses a wheelchair. In the community, you might draw children's attention to the fact that there is

no safe way to cross the street to get to the park or to the lack of diversity in the dolls and puzzles that are offered in the school or available in the local toy store.

2. *Discuss potential activism with the children.* Guide them in exploring their ideas and feeling about the fairness of the situation and what might be done to make it fairer. Assess the children's interest and the possibilities for action that are appropriate to their ages and skills.

3. *Work with children to design actions that are safe and workable from your perspective.* Examples of children taking action reflect a range of issues. When children in a community college child development center noticed the lack of diversity in the images of children in a new calendar, their teacher helped them write a letter to the company. When the company did not respond, the children circulated a petition around the college. At another center, racist slurs appeared on a wall in a nearby playground used by the children. The children and their teacher discussed what to do and painted over the hurtful words. In a parent-cooperative preschool, the children, with their teacher's help, made signs asking people not to litter in their favorite park. A first-grade class wrote letters to the local newspaper about the closure of a local library. In an early childhood special education program, the children put "tickets" on cars parked illegally in their school's handicapped parking spots. (For a fuller discussion of the process for generating and implementing emergent activism projects, see Hoffman, 2004 and Pelo & Davidson, 2000.)

Help children appreciate that ordinary people working together can make a positive difference in their lives. There are now some excellent children's books for 4- and 5-year-olds about children engaged in actions that remedy unfair situations in their immediate environments. (See list in Appendix A.)

With 5- to 8-year-olds, widen the focus to include activism to improve the lives of children in the larger community. As issues come up in the community, talk to children about them and see what strikes their interest. For example, children might write and visit municipal officials to press to have swings, slides, and play areas added to a park that is close to a poor neighborhood. At this age they may also be interested in raising money for people in more distant areas who are suffering particular hardships such as those caused by civil war or natural disasters.

Invite local activists, including members of children and staff's families, to talk about what they are doing. Remember that activism takes many forms, including cultural work such as community art and children's theater. White people and people of color work on campaigns to eliminate racial prejudice and discrimination through many educational and faith-based initiatives. These "unsung s/heroes" often have rich stories to tell, which help children see activists as real people. Be sure that the message is not about "rescuing" others but rather about the power and impact of people working together to make positive changes. Children can share these stories with their families by documenting the visits of local activists and making books or chart stories.

Familiarize school-age children with the history of resistance to injustice in our country that has been carried on by activists of all backgrounds, including whites. Knowing about white anti-racism activists is essential to white children's building a new white identity. However, there is very little material for children on this topic. In fact, because this information is excluded from mainstream textbooks, you may need to build your own knowledge about anti-racism activism. One way to begin is to learn more about the people whom we talk about in Chapter 6 and who are listed in Appendix C. With Internet resources, this information is much more readily available than it was only a few years ago. Learning about these activists and the movements in which they were or are participating will lead you to other people and resources. You can then turn this information into stories to share with the children. In these stories, be sure to emphasize the collective nature of activism and the importance of ordinary people's involvement, as well as the roles of leaders. Be sure to include examples of whites participating in organizations and movements that are led by people of color. Send book ideas to publishers and urge that they encourage authors to write stories about past and current activists.

In this chapter we have offered strategies and examples for supporting the development of children's empathic awareness of racial and cultural diversity, critical thinking, and activism. It is a challenge to make these skills and issues meaningful to young children, but by weaving these themes into all parts of your program, they will become part of children's earliest orientations to their social worlds. They will learn to value this work, not because it is something "nice" for others, but because it engenders a more satisfying and powerful way to live.

CHAPTER 9

Cultivating Caring and Activism with Staff and Families

Being an anti-racist is not founded on what racist attitudes a person doesn't have but rather is based on what anti-racist ideas, goals, and actions one takes part in to combat racism. So, for me this concept of anti-racist has been a very liberating one.
—Pacific Oaks student, in L. Derman-Sparks and C. B. Phillips, *Teaching/Learning Anti-racism: A Developmental Approach*

This chapter builds on the work with staff and families that we described in Chapter 5. As with curriculum for children, it is best to begin by having adults explore their own racial and cultural identities before moving on to a larger view of the human family. The learning themes in this chapter focus on activism and are especially pertinent to the adage "Children do as adults do, not as they say."

ADDRESSING THE LEARNING THEMES WITH ADULTS

The goals of working with adults parallel those we described for children in Chapter 8. One desired outcome is that white adults will examine their own misinformation and prejudices toward people of color, gain accurate knowledge, and broaden their range of relationships. Another hope is that with these skills and more in-depth knowledge about the inequities of our society, staff and families will work to create possibilities for all people to equitably share the resources in their communities, our country, and the world.

Needless to say, some families may resist the idea of becoming activists or of their children taking on such a role. They may be perfectly comfortable with the status quo, see no reason to become involved, and dismiss activists as destructive troublemakers. Alternatively, they may feel vulnerable and afraid that they might lose their job, their housing, or the respect of their community or religious group if they dare to rock the boat. To engage families, we need to help them see the connection between their dreams for their children and making their school, community, and the broader world a more sustainable and equitable place. For instance, persuading the city to allocate more funds to early childhood programs will result in a better future for all residents; taking a stand against the polluting practices of a local company will create a healthier environment for everyone's children.

As you consider the ideas for working with staff and families in this chapter, you may want to review the phases of adult anti-racist identity development described in Chapter 1. This information may help you to think about how you have changed, how you might want to change, and how to guide reflections and discussions with families and staff. Doing AB/MC work with adults is like eating an artichoke—it is necessary to peel off one layer at a time, and the amount of substance on each layer gets greater as you get closer to the heart—the place where change can happen. It should be remembered, however, that to get to the heart of an artichoke, you first have to get rid of the white fuzzy hairs, which taste terrible and can be difficult to remove.

LEARNING ABOUT YOURSELF

The following questions will help you reflect on your views related to people beyond your immediate family, circle of friends, and colleagues and on your engagement (or lack thereof) in social activism. As we explained in Chapter 5, engaging in continuing self-reflection will strengthen you to work with children and families.

These questions also can be adapted to inspire and inform small-group discussions among staff and families. Getting to know one another's experiences and views will lead to topics for further learning together. But first, ask yourself the following questions:

- Over the past 5 years, how much contact have I had with individuals and groups from backgrounds different from mine and in what situations and roles? How have I felt in these situations?
- Of the people who are part of my daily life (family members, closest friends, colleagues, family physician, mentors, clergy, supervisors, supervisees), how many are white? How many are from a cultural, language, or social-class background that is

different from mine? How truly diverse is my immediate world? Do I want to change the balance?

- When I meet or work with a family with a very different cultural lifestyle from mine, how do I react? Do I want to "educate" them to live more as I do? How open am I to learning about their lives and using that knowledge to reflect on my own choices and values?

- What stereotypes about people based on race, religion, language, or culture do I know? Which stereotypes do I hold? (Just write what comes to mind without self-censuring. Remember that all of us learn the stereotypes that pervade our society, even if we do not agree with them. You may surprise yourself with how many you know.) How do these stereotypes affect my initial perception of people? When I watch a movie or television show or read the newspaper, how conscious am I of stereotyped roles and messages? Are there some stereotypes that I notice more than others?

- How do I react when my assumptions about different groups are contradicted by new information? Do I dismiss it as just an exception to the rule? Do I notice it, feel good about it, and then file it away without further thought? Do I use the experience as an opportunity to rethink my original assumptions?

- How do I feel when others stereotype my own racial, cultural, or religious group? How do I respond? What keeps me from acting? What helps me to act?

- How do I feel when I hear or see others (family, friends, or coworkers) disrespect others, make prejudiced remarks, or act in discriminatory ways? What do I do? What keeps me from acting? What helps me to act?

- How do I feel when I hear children making stereotypical or negative comments about people's identity? How comfortable am I talking with children about their ideas and attitudes? What are the sources of any discomfort I may feel?

- If I knew from this point on that every person on the planet would have adequate shelter, food, and clothing forever, how would I feel? How would this change my views about material goods? My perceptions of other people? How would a more equitable distribution of wealth affect my life?

- Who or what do I think is responsible for the disparities in wealth? What (if anything) do I think should be done about these inequities?

- What role does consumption (shopping, looking through catalogs, watching infomercials) play in my life? How do I feel when

I purchase something new or cannot buy something I would like to have? Do I consider the environmental impact or disparities in resource distribution when I think about buying a new item or planning a trip? How aware am I of different companies' labor and environmental practices? How does this information (or lack of it) influence what I buy?

- When I think of doing anti-bias and anti-racist work, what images of being an activist come to mind? Where do these images come from? Direct experience? My education? The media?
- Do I think of myself as an activist? If not, why not? If yes, what experiences have I had as an activist that can help me to do AB/MC work? What values/behaviors in my family's history support my being an anti-bias/anti-racist activist? Which ones make it difficult?
- Which social activists—from any group and any historical period—are potential role models for me? Why? Which of their attributes and activities are most appealing? Least appealing?

LEARNING ABOUT YOUR CHILDREN'S FAMILIES

Approach the process of gathering information as shared explorations, not as interrogations ("I would like to learn more about your child's and family's experiences so I can do a better job of being her teacher"). Often family members feel reassured if you also talk about your own experiences, especially about times when you have felt uncomfortable talking about racial issues and blunders that you have made in these conversations. If people start to become uncomfortable or resistant, then back off a bit and shift to another focus (if a parent is reluctant to talk about the racial composition of the community, he/she might be willing to talk about its different religious groups, which may be very informative). This flexibility does not mean abandoning the conversation but rather finding a more effective approach.

The following questions are only suggestions and should be adapted for specific groups. Hopefully, they will act as catalysts for more extended conversations.

- What is your community like? Who lives there? What racial, ethnic, or religious groups are there? Where do people work? What kinds of jobs do they have?
- How much contact has your family had, and, in particular, have your children had, with people from other racial, cultural,

religious, and social-class groups? How have they responded to differences?

- Have your children asked questions or made comments about race? About poverty? About someone with an unfamiliar accent or a disability? If so, what have they said? How have you responded?
- With what institutions are your children familiar (workplaces, churches, stores, the welfare system)? What is the racial composition in those institutions? What messages do you think your children are learning about which groups hold different types of jobs? What have they learned about which groups are in authority and which ones hold more subordinate positions?
- What messages about race, culture, and social class do you think your children are learning from the television programs that they watch? Books that they read? Have you and your children ever had conversations about these messages? What are some of the questions or reactions they have expressed?
- What do you want your child to learn about racial and ethnic diversity?

STRATEGIES FOR WORKING WITH FAMILIES AND STAFF

Since the strategies we describe in this chapter build on those described in Chapter 5, they are usually best introduced after you have done some work on the first three learning themes. The ideas described in this section can be applied to a wide range of people, those who are just beginning to consider these issues and those who are at the later phases of their anti-racism journey. What will vary is people's depth of discussion and willingness to take action on specific issues. As you learn about family and staff members' experiences with racial and cultural diversity and where they are in their anti-racist identity journey, you will be able to tailor activities to meet their specific needs. As we stressed in Chapter 5, you need to be open to many different ways in which people respond. See your role as generating interest, providing information, and encouraging—but not forcing—people to stretch and take risks. Respect participants' unique histories and perspectives and the different paths they will take.

Implementing Learning Theme Four

The following activities complement and support those for the classroom that are described in Chapter 8, which focus on expanding children's awareness, appreciation, and respect for people beyond their immediate world. In addition, these activities can stimulate people to begin to recognize and challenge the invisible norm of whiteness that underlies our social and economic structures and many of our personal decisions. In many cases, work with families and work with children can be merged into a single project.

Explore ways that families can expand their experience with people of color. Most communities have more diversity than many whites realize. Encourage families to identify specific ways they can build connections with individual people of color in the larger community, (joining an integrated place of worship, building a relationship between two places of worship, getting to know people through participating in cultural or social-action groups, seeking out professional people of color such as a pediatrician or dentist, being committed to building a more diverse staff in the center). Note that employing a person of color as a gardener or housekeeper does not meet the spirit of this guideline, because typically people in these jobs are treated as subordinate to the family, which reinforces messages of white superiority.

Help families consider how they might bring racial and cultural diversity into their home environments, as you are doing in the classroom. Encourage families to provide materials (such as skin-tone supplies for art projects) and children's books and toys with characters and stories that reflect a range of ethnic and cultural groups within the United States. Ask families to help you create a lending or exchange library in your center with books, toys, cassette tapes, videos, and CDs that authentically represent a wide range of people. Encourage families to build more diversity into their own library, art, and music.

Invite family members to observe children's questions and comments about diversity and discuss ways to address them. To stimulate interest in this activity, you may want to document questions and comments you hear from the children and use these as a starting place. Ask family members to bring one of their children's comments and post it on a wall chart. When you have several of these comments, they can become the basis of a discussion with interested families.

Organize conversations with local leaders and activists of color who can directly describe issues that children and families in the community face. This personal contact often catches people's attention and motivates further learning and possible involvement in changing unjust conditions, as we saw in Krista's story in Chapter 1.

Organize discussion groups focused on books and articles that tell authentic stories or experiences of individual people and families. There are many excellent novels written by people of color (Julia Alvarez, Bebe Moore Campbell, Toni Morrison, and Amy Tang, to name just a few) that draw white readers into new perspectives and help them to see that their way of life is only one of many realities in the United States. As important, they illuminate the effects of racism and help whites recognize their unconscious racist assumptions and actions.

Implementing Learning Theme Five

Again, paralleling the work with children, you can help adults learn to identify stereotypes and the pain that they cause. In addition, you can facilitate the development of their skills for challenging prejudicial and discriminatory behavior as well as teaching their children how to do this.

Have staff and family members talk about their childhood experiences of being teased, humiliated, or rejected because of some aspect of their identity. Use their stories as a bridge to addressing the racism directed at people of color. Facilitate discussions in which participants explore how these experiences have affected their feelings about themselves and others. Perhaps in conjunction with books or videos, use those experiences to help participants identify with the pain of discrimination suffered by people of color. These discussions may also lead to ideas about participants' hopes for how their children treat others. If participants believe that children are "color blind," you can talk to them about research (including the reviews in Chapters 3 and 7) that shows how readily young children notice race and absorb common prejudices. To bring the discussion closer to home, you can also present examples (with identities completely disguised, of course) from your program that illustrate children's discomfort and stereotypes about people of color.

Explore staff/family members' stereotypes of different racial and ethnic groups and how these influence their attitudes and behaviors about those groups. Pass out index cards and ask people to describe stereotypes they have learned or heard (without identifying themselves) and place the cards in a bowl. Read the cards out loud or list their contents on easel paper. Ask people to talk in dyads about how they learned these stereotypes. Then, in the whole group, talk about how stereotypes harm everyone and how people can unlearn their prejudices.

Involve participants in critiquing popular children's films, television programs, and books for stereotypes and misinformation. Ask family members to keep records of the stereotypes in programs and ads on television that their children regularly watch and are exposed to. Bring in a selection of children's books that contain stereotypical messages and ask staff/family members to critique these. (See "Ten Quick Ways . . ." in the Anti-bias Curriculum book [Derman-Sparks et al., 1989].) In addition, collect and critique elements found in holiday decorations and greeting cards, among the most obvious being images of Native Americans that are portrayed in the Thanksgiving context. (See Bisson, 1997, for further examination of holiday issues from an anti-bias perspective). Describe the strategies you are using to teach children how to recognize and resist stereotypes and explore how families might use them at home.

Implementing Learning Theme Six

The following set of strategies dovetails with related classroom activities about caring for the resources of the earth. As children and their families become more mindful of the environment and the unequal distribution of material resources, they can work together to make changes in the classroom, in their homes, and in the community.

Invite family and staff members to talk about ways that they feel pressured by consumerism and its effects on their children. Be alert to issues that are on families' minds. For example, as the holidays approach in November and December, many families feel that they have to purchase the latest expensive toys, clothes, and sports equipment for their children. They often feel torn between financial constraints and the barrage of mesmerizing commercials directed at their children. Brainstorm ways to counter the pressures on their children and themselves. For example, plan a joint school-family project in which you work together to make needed learning materials for the school or where family members make a book about themselves for their children.

Facilitate a discussion or workshop to talk about families' goals for their children and their child-rearing values related to possessions. You might invite the families to join an evening conversation on the theme "How Much Is Enough?" This event might provide a timely opportunity for families to share their concerns and think about ways to put more emphasis on caring connections with the family rather than on material things. Ask families to brainstorm activities they already do that do not involve buying new and expensive objects for their children (a family day in a local park or zoo, a family dinner where everyone cooks together, a day during the vacation that their child plans)

Pay attention to families' socioeconomic realities and tailor discussion questions for the range of income within your group. For relatively affluent families, you might pose the idea that they collectively commit themselves to buying less for their children. They can mutually support efforts to counteract their children's arguments about how much everyone else is getting and resist gift-giving pressures from members of their extended families. As an alternative to purchasing expensive gifts or throwing lavish birthday parties, families can learn about social justice and charitable organizations and choose one or two to support. Engaging children in these conversations and decisions exposes them to the hardships of many people and enables them to participate in organizational and individual efforts to achieve more equity. For lower-income families, agreeing that they will not succumb to the competitive pressures is also important, as well as brainstorming strategies to provide gifts that are within their income range. Familiarize all families with children's books that address ways lower-income family members show their love for one another (e.g., *A Chair for My Mom* and *The Patchwork Quilt*—see Appendix A for list).

Involve families in environmental activities that contribute to the school and to the community's improvement. Tending a school garden and setting up recycling programs are a few of the many environmental projects that can be done collaboratively with families, children, and staff. Pelo and Davidson (2000) describe how families and schools can also work on community projects such as planting and caring for trees in a neighborhood park or creating a community garden.

Raise people's awareness about environmental-justice issues in the city and state. While many people may know about efforts to preserve wildlife and habitats, they may not be as aware of issues that particularly affect working-class and poor communities, such as lead pollution, proliferation of waste-disposal plants, nuclear-waste dumps, or poorly ventilated factories. Collect material from national environmental-justice organizations and invite local activists from these groups to talk about their work. Out of these meetings, further ideas for discussion and activities may emerge.

Expand consciousness of national and global environmental and consumerism issues. Read and discuss "What Do Trees Have to Do with Peace?", the story of the environmental work of Dr. Wangari Maathai, the 2004 recipient of the Nobel Peace Prize (see Appendix D). Videos are also a useful tool for stimulating further thinking about the interactive relationships between the environment, consumerism, race, class, peace, and democracy. (For example, "The Global Banquet: Politics of Food," 2001, which examines how American food choices affect the environment and worldwide economy, and "The Child Behind the Label", 1995, which looks at how child laborers produce goods bought by Americans. Both can be purchased though Teaching for Change (See Appendix B).

Implementing Learning Theme Seven

Acquiring skills and confidence to work for social justice in our schools, in our communities, and in the larger society and world are integral to AB/MC work. In this section we suggest several strategies for engaging families in social change.

Explore images of activism that family and staff members hold. Being an activist has a range of meanings for people, many hold stereotypical images based on distorted media representations. As a starting place, invite family members and staff to share the images/key words that define activism for them. Reflect together on the authenticity of these images and words.

Think about the meaning of citizenship in a democratic society and the value of "ordinary" people taking responsibility to act in the face of injustice. Ask people to relate stories about their own, family members', neighbors', and friends' participation in social-justice work.

Involve families in children's action projects (see Chapter 8).

Learn about the stories of ordinary people who have worked or are working for racial justice. Go to the Web site Voices of Civil Rights, which is a joint project of the American Association of Retired People (AARP), the Leadership Conference on Civil Rights, and the Library of Congress. This Web site has wonderful stories from people throughout the United States (see Appendix B). You can also invite local social-justice activists to talk about their experiences. Families and staff can work together to create teaching materials for the children based on these stories.

Encourage staff and families to collaborate on addressing pressing AB/MC concerns in the school and in the community. To generate interest and participation, display information about local and national social-justice movements and organize car pools to specific local events. Recognize families who take action by posting this information on the family bulletin board or including it in class and school newsletters. At the school level, invite families and staff to work together to assemble and make materials that will bring greater diversity to the program's environment. At the community level, they could work with local libraries, toy stores, and bookstores to help develop a wider range of diversity in their selections; they could also get involved in actions to pressure the town to provide more services for low-income residents. Participants who are interested in politics might investigate and challenge local inequities and state and federal policies that create or perpetuate them. Check out the Web site of the Civil Rights Coalition for the 21st Century for current information and links to several other national groups (See Appendix B).

NEXT STEPS: INVESTIGATING RACISM AS A SYSTEM

To take AB/MC work with adults to the next level requires studying how the system of racism operates in our country. Although it may not be realistic to go further with all your families and staff, some individuals may be interested in meeting more regularly to engage in this study. We also strongly urge you to find ways to continue your own study (see the resources in Appendices B and C). Here are a few strategies you can use with staff and families who wish to take the next steps in their anti-racism and social-justice journey.

Gain a broader perspective of United States history. To engage your group in this process, suggest that as a group, you read aloud the dramatic readings in Howard Zinn's book *The People Speak* (2004), a collection of diverse voices telling stories that applaud the enduring spirit of dissent throughout the history of the United States. For people who enjoy reading, assign various chapters of Ronald Takaki's *A Different Mirror* (1993), a portrait of the history of several different ethnic groups. Then ask each person or small group to report to the whole group. To explore the topic of what information was not part of their regular education, see James Lowen's *Lies My Teacher Told Me* (1995) and *Lies Across America: What Our Historical Sites Get Wrong* (1999).

Learn about the history of the construction of "whiteness" and how it has affected different groups. Study the construction of whiteness and its impact on various European ethnic groups (see Allen, 1994; Brodkin, 1998

[Jewish identity]; Ignatiev, 1995 [Irish identity]). Ask participants to consider what it would mean to them if the current social-political construct of "whiteness" no longer existed. How might this shift affect how they think about themselves? How might it change how they live their lives?

Learn about the dynamics of systemic racism. One excellent resource for opening up this topic is a video titled *Ending Racism: Working for a Racism Free 21st Century*. Made by Crossroads Ministry, an interfaith, community-based, anti-racism education and training organization, it comes with a detailed discussion guide. (See Appendix B for contact information). For the group that enjoys reading, Paul Kivel's *Uprooting Racism: How White People Can Work for Racial Justice* (2002) is a reader-friendly book that will open up many growth-producing discussions.

Learn about past and current white anti-racist activists. Start with the list in Appendix C and read more about them in the cited references. Also use the information in the Voices of Civil Rights project that we previously mentioned.

Explore staff/families' visions of a society free of racism (and other isms). After the establishment of an analysis of systemic racism, an additional strategy is to explore people's visions of a society free of racism (and other isms). In small groups of 4–5 people, ask participants to envision a child-care center, a school, or a community health-care system in which there are no barriers to accessibility and quality because of a person's limited resources or race or cultural background. Ask everyone to put aside all preconceived ideas and limitations and assume they have a free hand and ample resources to create these new institutions. Then, ask each group to relate their ideas and to describe their feelings as they imagine living in such a society. End by suggesting that they hold on to their ideas and feelings as you all work toward improving your own program and community. (You can also repeat this activity, focusing on eliminating class or gender or sexual-orientation inequities.) Follow up this exercise by identifying specific changes people would like to work toward in their child-care program, in schools, and in their communities.

Form or join a support/action group. Because AB/MC work is complex, teachers or families who try to go it alone may end up feeling discouraged and stop trying. Experienced AB/MC educators and activists often credit their networks for enabling them to go from being bystanders to taking action and for staying involved for the long haul (Alvarado et al., 1999).

Support groups provide opportunities for participants to deepen their knowledge about racism and other isms, to find and give support for personal changes, and to continue to develop new ways of thinking and acting in their work and communities.

Some support/action groups are program based, with families and teachers meeting regularly (weekly, biweekly, or monthly) to discuss their own experiences and ways to build AB/MC work in their school. One teacher called her school support group a "Circle of Girlfriends" (Annette Unten in Alvarado et al., 1999). Others prefer to organize or join support groups made up of teachers and community people outside of the center or school, perhaps through a local AEYC or other professional organization, or a faith-based or community organization. In the absence of local support groups, teachers have formed chat rooms or e-mail discussion groups to have a place to express their concerns and to get feedback and support.

Support groups require a long-term commitment and regular attendance, so that members can build trust and learn how to productively navigate the challenges of examining race and racism and of developing anti-racist relationships, child-rearing strategies, and schools and communities. Discussion topics are determined by group members' experiences, interests, and ideas about where they need to grow. Storytelling and analysis of the themes that arise from the stories are the most common methods, often supplemented with discussions about books, videos, and invited speakers. Successful support/action groups find it is most productive to balance discussions related to personal growth with those focused on ways to take action in their school and community.

Certain group dynamics can derail discussions about race and racism, even among dedicated people. For example, some support-group members may feel superior to others because they see themselves as being "further along" in dealing with racial issues. To have open discussions, people must put aside their feelings of competitiveness and superiority and listen to themselves and others with openness and humility. They need to understand that no one is ever free of the effects of racism and that every conversation is an opportunity to deepen understanding of how racism has influenced their lives and the larger society.

Another trap is the acting out of power differentials, reflecting the lines of gender, social class, or race in our society or in a hierarchal relationship between teachers and families. When these appear, use them as "teachable moments" to further examine how these social-political constructs undermine the creation of equitable relationships. Finally, fear of conflict or discomfort is another potentially derailing dynamic.

Racism is, in its essence, hurtful and dehumanizing. Undoing it—whether in ourselves, our families, or our early childhood programs—can also be painful—even while it is humanizing and liberating. Learning how to manage conflict enables group members to express disagreements and to hear and understand the complexities of multiple perspectives. (For ideas about creating and maintaining support/action groups, see Chang et al., 2000, and Cronin et al., 1998.)

Ultimately, AB/MC work "is a path where we walk in companionship. . . . And through these relationships . . . [we] realize that no one does this work alone, that they travel with friends and . . . a 'suitcase full of hope'" (Alvarado et al., 1997, p. 210).

> I think it's because, in untying the knot [of racism and other isms], you're unraveling the web of lies that each of us has inevitably experienced [and] that have taken their dehumanizing toll. . . . In unraveling even a bit of the whole, we feel tremendously excited. We have only to unravel a bit of it to reclaim ourselves more completely. (Early childhood educator quoted in Derman-Sparks & Phillips, 1997, p. 127)

A Tale of Two Centers

EPISODE TWO

Episode 2 of the centers' narratives illustrates how the teachers implemented aspects of Learning Themes 4 through 7.

THE MOTHER JONES CENTER

In the first episode, the children had made books on the theme "Everyone Works in My Family." The teachers wanted to build on the children's enthusiasm about the topic to expand their ideas about families and work beyond their immediate experience (Learning Theme 4). At circle time the teachers made charts with the children showing how lots of tasks are shared by all families and the many ways families get their work done. Multiracial persona dolls were used to broaden the range of family approaches and jobs—which led to an unexpected and troubling conversation. One of the persona dolls, Samantha, was depicted as African American, and her daddy as a schoolteacher. Adding Samantha to the chart, Liz asked the children, "And what do you think Samantha's daddy does to help his family?" One of the children said, "He's a garbage man." The other children nodded. Liz, taken aback, said, "No, he's a teacher. He teaches third grade." The children shook their heads. "Unh unh," said Bradley firmly. "Black guys pick up the garbage."

Liz didn't know what to say. In fact, in their neighborhood, the only African American men most of the children had contact with did indeed collect the garbage. Even the school garbage was collected by two African American men. It was clear that the curriculum needed to be broadened, but Liz was not sure how to do it.

After talking it over, Liz, Charlie, and Marina decided that if they couldn't find more people of color to bring into the children's lives, they could at least be sure the children got to know those few who were in the community and to dispel children's assumptions based on their limited information (Learning Themes 4 and 5). They decided to have the children interview the center's support staff, most of whom were people of color, to get to know them as individuals. They arranged for the children to interview the school secretary, the cook, and the mail carrier. It took some major arrangements to get one of the garbage collectors to come to school, but when he did, he became an instant hero, as he also brought the huge truck and showed the children how it lifted up the dumpster and crushed the trash. The teachers invited him to talk about his children (aged 3, 5, and 9), and his hobby (fixing motorcycles). After each visit the children gave the people they interviewed a bouquet of "flowers" made at the art table and followed up with a thank-you letter. The teachers put the information the children had gathered into a book with a snapshot of each person, which they added to their "Everybody Works" collection.

Wanting to broaden the "Everybody Works" curriculum, and to address the incipient racism inherent in the children's lack of contact with people of color, the staff moved on to a curriculum they named "We Are All the Same— We Are All Different" (Learning Themes 2 and 4). They decided to first strengthen the children's exploration and sense of comfort with the differences within the classroom and within their neighborhoods and increase their sense of comfort with talking about differences and similarities.

To encourage the children to really *see* one another, Marina made a matching game with digital photos of the backs of children's heads and of their faces. She was surprised by how easily the children identified slight differences, such as the length of a boy's hair, or the degree of wave in a child's hair. At circle they made "eye charts," counting how many people had blue, green, hazel, or brown eyes and how many wore glasses. The classroom persona dolls extended the conversations and were included in all the charting. One of the dolls, Pilar, wore glasses, and the children helped her solve the problem of children teasing her about the glasses.

The curriculum continued to build with ideas such as "Everybody sleeps, but we sleep in different places" (shared beds, bunk beds, cribs, hammocks, mats on the floor, with grandparents, alone in a bed). "Everybody eats but we eat different foods" (all the different kinds of breakfasts children have, who gets to drink coffee and who does not, the different ways that people make bread and other pastries).

Charlie, Liz, and Marina also began to discuss what they could do to build a caring community among the families (Learning Theme 3 and 5). To prepare for this, the three teachers talked about specific families with whom they were struggling. Of particular concern was the Curtis family. JoAnn Curtis never seemed to be able to "get it together." She was inevitably late, dragging her twins in to school still in their pajamas at 9:30 or 10:00. She rarely returned forms on time (or at all) and never participated in the parent meetings.

Liz, who had been silent through most of the meeting, finally spoke up. "I know how hard it is," she said. "I remember when I was working and going to school and the kids were little. It's hard when your car breaks down and you have no money to fix it. The buses are unreliable and crowded and noisy and never run when you need them. I used to be so ashamed to show up at parent meetings because I could never get there on time, and I couldn't talk the way the other parents did." She fell silent again. Marina and Charlie looked at each other feeling embarrassed and ashamed. Charlie said slowly, "You know I have to say that I had not thought about it from that perspective. I had only been thinking about my own annoyance and the inconvenience it has caused for us. Let's try to figure out how *we* can help her get the twins here on time." Marina nodded and said, "What about keeping some clothes for the twins here, so that we can change them if they need to come in their pajamas?" Charlie agreed, "Good idea. Also, lets see if there are any parents who live near her who might be able to help with transportation."

There was a pause, and then Marina turned to Liz and said softly "Are you afraid to talk to us?" (She was indicating Charlie and herself.) "Sometimes," Liz admitted. "You're both so educated. You're really intelligent and I feel . . . sort of dumb sometimes." The teachers were silent for a few moments and then Charlie said, "I wonder how many of our kids are learning that they aren't 'intelligent' too? I think you're brilliant, Liz. I wish you shared more of your thinking. I mean, look at how you turned around that first parent meeting!"

During the first parent meeting, the teachers had asked the families to talk to one another about their goals for their children during the school year. The conversation had not gone well. Many of the participants were silent, and those who spoke were focused on the issues they themselves had struggled with in the elementary schools. "I want her to learn to pay attention." "I want him to learn to read and write." "I want the kids to learn not to get into trouble." "He can't sit still." Charlie was disgusted that the families didn't have "age-appropriate goals." Marina felt discouraged that there were some parents who seemed to have no goals at all for their children. Liz, however, suddenly spoke up and began to talk about what it had been like for her as a low-income single mother putting her children through school. She talked about pressuring her children to "stay clean" no matter what, remembering her own childhood experience of being teased because of her old, dirty clothes. Now that her children were older, she divulged, she regretted not letting them play freely and putting so much pressure on them. She then asked the family members to go into groups of three and talk about experiences in their own childhoods that they wanted to protect their children from. The conversation was lively and intense. The teachers then talked a little about how they saw the center curriculum providing strength for the children and skills for healthy survival. Liz brought the conversation back to the participants and asked them what qualities in their families they most wanted to pass on to their children. And that became the list of "values" that the teachers wrote down and posted in their classrooms.

Despite the successful outcome of the first meeting, it was clear to the three teachers that tensions and distrust continued to exist between the families. Those parents who were working seemed hostile to those on public subsidy. The student parents sought one another out and appeared to avoid the other families. Some of the parents who were employed made critical comments (often in front of the children) about the "welfare families" who "took" their tax dollars, and they were uneasy about their children playing with "*those* kids, from *those* families." The staff wondered how much of this was being transmitted to the children.

While the staff was thinking through what they wanted to do, three of the mothers asked to meet with them. Nervously, but very firmly, the women informed the teachers that they did not want their children playing with food. The cornmeal table, the bean collages, the macaroni necklaces could feed their families for a week. "Food is for eating," one of the mom's said sternly, "not for wasting." Chagrined, the teachers agreed at once to stop using food for curriculum projects, and as they discussed their obliviousness to the issue, they also began to discuss the amount of wasted food at snack and lunchtime. After the staff meeting the teachers thought the food-wasting issue might be something that could build bridges for all the families. They decided to launch a compost plan and plant a small garden. Parents agreed to help build planter boxes and seek donations of small tools and good dirt; a compost box was put up in the yard (Learning Theme 6).

The children were fascinated with the project. Watching food scraps turn to dirt was as interesting as watching seeds sprout. Everyone was also entranced by the seedlings; the teachers had to set limits on the children's enthusiasm to water the plants. The children could hardly wait until the lettuce and carrots came up.

As family members began to help in the school garden, they also began to eye the vacant lot down the block from the school. Planting in boxes was fine, but planting in the ground would be a lot better. In the ground the children could grow strawberries. Perhaps families could have their own plots and grow their own vegetables—or even flowers! A small delegation of the parents got together, for the first time working across the lines of difference between them. They researched the ownership of the lot and found it could be for sale. No one had enough money, but Charlie thought that if they gathered enough neighbors together perhaps they could get the city to lease the lot as a community garden (Learning Themes 6 and 7).

Excitement ran high as family members organized a newsletter, set up a petition, arranged for their county supervisor to make a visit. The petition was displayed in front of the school with a bulletin board of pictures of the children working in the garden and with copies of some of their artwork. Many neighbors began dropping in to the school to see what the children were doing and to offer small supplies (a pair of garden gloves, some sweet-pea seeds, a tube of sunscreen).

Meanwhile, it occurred to Marina that the garden might be a tie to the a nearby community of Central American farmworkers. After careful discussion with Liz and Charlie, a new curriculum was born: "Food—Where Does It Come From?" The children went on field trips to see who planted the strawberry fields, who picked the strawberries. How did the strawberries get from the fields to the store? Who took care of the food in the store? And of course, how do strawberries taste?!

Marina felt that things were going very well, until she heard Bradley say to Michael, "We're going to visit those aliens tomorrow!" Stunned, she asked Bradley what he thought an alien was. "You know," he replied, "those brown people from Mars who pick the strawberries." Checking with the morning teachers, she discovered that some of the parents had been uneasy about the field trips. There had been conversations about "illegal aliens" and some anger from parents with family members who had lost their union jobs when the frozen-food plant was transferred to Mexico.

The three teachers decided to address these issues directly with the families and called a meeting (Learning Theme 5); Liz facilitated, with the support of Marina and Charlie. Speaking as a member of the neighborhood, Liz led a discussion about how people often scorn and mistreat farm workers who are often very poor. She named these attitudes and behaviors as stereotypes, misinformation, and social oppression. From there, she and Marina began to talk about the conditions of the families who worked in the fields. They made the connections between the struggles that many of the center families were having and the struggles of the farmworker families.

Not all the parents were convinced. However, when Charlie began to talk about the children's misinformation regarding "aliens," "garbage men," and "dirty skin" and the emotional pain that these terms inflict on people, most of the parents were concerned and wanted to learn more. Together parents and teachers identified ways that children had absorbed these biased assumptions from what they saw (and did not see!) in their community and in the media. They then brainstormed ideas for challenging the negative images and conveying more accurate ones. Ideas began to flow and a new curriculum focus began to emerge.

And so the work continues . . .

THE LOUISA MAY ALCOTT CENTER

In the first episode, the teachers had implemented several changes to try to curb the children's competitiveness, which seemed to reflect their families' white privilege and desire to raise superstar children. After several weeks of emphasizing cooperative activities and encouraging the children to learn about their similarities and differences, Brenda and Vera noticed that the competition among the children had abated somewhat. Family members seemed more relaxed and less worried about their children's accomplishments. Still, a tone of entitlement continued to pervade the conversations, which often revolved around exotic vacations, expensive purchases, and seemingly unlimited budgets for children's activities. The teachers were struck with how many families seemed to live in a bubble of restless affluence—never questioning their right to use as many resources as they could afford, yet never feeling satisfied. Brenda, from her perspective of having grown up in a working-class family, felt that there was an "invisible norm of affluence" that was going unquestioned in the classroom.

To tackle this issue, the teachers built on the discussions they had already initiated about how resources were often distributed unequally and decided to make these differences more real to the children. In the classroom they took a step beyond the cooperative activities and set up situations of scarcity (a small numbers of markers, a single pair of scissors) that required the children to wait, negotiate, and share. As they talked through the frustrations and conflicts that arose in these situations, the teachers introduced carefully selected pictures and stories that depicted people from many different groups (including whites) living in less advantaged circumstances (Learning themes 4 and 6). The teachers challenged the children to consider how they might feel if they were living with very few resources.

Although the children were interested and concerned, a couple of them also made comments about poor people being lazy. The teachers were concerned that children were absorbing negative stereotypes about poor people and had no idea of what it really meant to be poor. They wanted to make poverty more real and meaningful to the children. Al, an old friend of Brenda's who worked at a homeless shelter, came to the classroom for several visits. He showed pictures and told the children about his work and about some of the families who lived in the shelter. The children asked a lot of questions about the families in the shelter, and several talked about how it was not fair that some kids did not have a place to live. A few parents expressed concern about their children being exposed to "such depressing" information, but others were impressed at their children's thoughtful comments and questions about poverty and homelessness.

The teachers decided to address the issues of entitlement and superiority head-on and planned a family–staff meeting to talk about them. They anticipated that this discussion would be difficult and invited a highly trained outside facilitator to run the meeting. The facilitator started the discussion by asking participants to list the stereotypes that people had about them and their jobs (sleazy lawyers, overpaid corrupt executives, pampered housewives) and to talk about how those made them feel. Then they asked participants to list (anonymously) on cards the stereotypes they had learned about different racial and income groups. Then the facilitator read the cards out loud and had participants talk in small groups about how they had learned those stereotypes and how they had influenced their attitudes about different groups. When the small groups were reporting out to the larger group, the conversation was lively, with some people talking about their feelings of embarrassment and guilt, while others reacted defensively (Learning Theme 5).

A pivotal moment came when Susan, a corporate lawyer, said quietly, "You know the problem isn't the poor people. The problem is that they don't have access to the resources and opportunities that we have. I hate to say this, but I think that maybe *we* are the problem." The conversation stopped and the room fell silent. The facilitator thanked Susan and used her comment to shift the conversation from personal guilt to thinking about changes that they could make in their own lives and ways that they could pressure institutions to address the larger systemic problems that underlie poverty (Learning Theme 6). Obviously, it was only the start of a very long conversation, but at the end of the meeting, many participants stayed behind to keep talking, and several asked to have some follow-up meetings.

Over the next few weeks, Brenda and Vera were pleased to notice that both children and family members begin to moderate their consumption patterns. For example, several family members mentioned that they had decided to forego lavish birthday parties and to have smaller, more simple events.

Meanwhile, to moderate children's fascination with new toys and games and to help them connect more closely with the natural environment, the teachers extended the time spent outdoors and used natural objects to teach concepts that they usually taught inside the classroom (counting trees, identifying leaf patterns). They also replaced some of the store-bought materials in the classroom with natural materials (grasses instead of paint brushes, twigs and small logs instead of blocks) to encourage children to appreciate the qualities of these materials and to invent new ways of working with them.

Vera's husband, an environmentalist, came to the school and talked to the children about local environmental problems. The children started to keep track of the amount of trash that accumulated in their classroom and came up with ways to cut down on waste (drawing and writing on both sides of the paper, using only one paper towel to dry their hands).

To make the connections between preserving the environment and the unequal consumption of resources more concrete, the teachers incorporated images and stories showing how people from different regions use and conserve the resources that they have (Learning Themes 4 and 6).

With the approaching holidays, the teachers organized a teacher-parent discussion group about the financial and social pressures that many families feel during the holidays. They began by having family members think about their favorite childhood memories. As people recalled special times with family and friends, they realized that very few of their happiest childhood moments had anything to do with new toys. Based on these memories, everyone brainstormed ideas about how to create enjoyable and meaningful family times that did not involve spending a lot of money.

A number of families decided to join forces to do some outdoor activities over the holidays (taking hikes, cleaning up a local park, skating and sliding on a nearby pond). Several families also decided to contribute some of the money they would have spent on presents to Al's homeless shelter. Some also arranged to volunteer at the shelter over the break. When school closed for the vacation, Brenda and Vera felt a glow of accomplishment. The children and families were beginning to let go of their competitiveness and sense of entitlement and were reaching out to one another and to the community in new ways.

When the children returned to school after the holidays, however, Brenda and Vera were dismayed to hear the old competitiveness take over the children's conversations. Despite the fact that a number of the families had tried to cut back on gifts, the children were bragging about what they had received for Christmas or Hanukkah, which, of course, sidelined the three children whose families did not observe either of these holidays. When the teachers mentioned these observations to the parents, they heard stories of relatives who piled on the gifts (despite the parents' efforts to shift the focus away from purchased presents) and of children watching many hours of television loaded with holiday commercials. Several of the parents seemed discouraged and ready to "just give in to the culture we can't do anything about it."

Vera and Brenda decided that it was time to move into a more activist phase so that parents and children would not be so overwhelmed by the cultural and economic forces that reinforced their consumerism and entitlement (Learning Theme 7). Since parents and children were both talking about television commercials, the teachers decided to start there. They asked the families to record the commercials that their children saw most frequently. Then they showed these clips to the children and helped them to talk about what the advertisers were saying and how they made the products look so enticing. The teachers also had the children think about the roles that boys and girls and people from different racial groups played in the commercials (Learning Theme 5). To provide contrasting images, the teachers brought back the photographs of families who had many fewer material goods.

Brenda and Vera also had an evening meeting at which they showed the tapes and contrasting images to the parents. Spurred on by this meeting, a number of parents investigated groups that were trying to get legislation passed that would limit or eliminate commercials directed at young children. As they visited Web sites and received literature from these groups, parents became aware of some of the racist practices of advertisers such as targeting specific racial groups for particular products (for example, pitching high-priced sneakers and alcoholic beverages to young African American men). Almost without realizing it, a number of parents turned the corner and became activists. They connected with different groups on the Internet and started to go to meetings and write letters to newspapers, broadcasting companies, and national and state legislators. The children participated by providing pictures and stories about how commercials were dishonest and stereotyped.

As they became more involved, parents began to see the connections between the poverty that they had discussed earlier and the deeper structural inequities that fueled hyperconsumption (sweatshops in poor countries, tax cuts that favored people such as themselves). As they learned more, a few parents began to question their personal priorities and the school admission and financial policies that effectively excluded children from lower-income families. Needless to say, these conversations made many family and staff members feel anxious and defensive, but they also forced people to begin to examine their roles in the larger social inequities.

As families began to understand the issues and join groups that were addressing them, they no longer felt helpless. Instead they felt energized and determined to use their political and economic clout to make a difference. Of course, not everyone participated, but those who did created an excited buzz at the school that kept people thinking and talking about their values and priorities. As with all AB/MC work, it was messy and often difficult, but it was also alive and daring and full of hope and enthusiasm.

And so the work continues . . .

Children's Books and Curriculum Resources

COMPILED BY LORI WATSON

Books provide excellent opportunities for children to explore their life experiences as well as the rich diversity of the many people on our planet. In a quality learning environment, children's literature enhances every child's sense of self and connections to the world.

However, books may expose children to misinformation about themselves and others. Therefore, adults must practice critical thinking. While a particular book may impressively address one aspect of diversity, it may also include stereotypical material about another aspect. We can decide to not select such a book, or we can use its flaws to nurture children's critical thinking. Furthermore, one book, even if excellent, can never depict the diversity within a group, so a range of stories and images are always necessary.

The following list is a starting place: we hope that you will regularly supplement it with books relevant to your specific setting. (See Appendix B for Web sites about children's literature.)

IDENTITY AND DIVERSITY AMONG WHITE CHILDREN AND FAMILIES

Adoff, Arnold. (1973). *Black is brown is tan*. New York: HarperCollins.
    A biracial family uses playful language to describe different skin colors
Bunting, E. (1991). *Fly away home*. New York: Clarion Books.
    A homeless family moves between airport terminals trying not to be noticed
Caseley, J. (1994). *Mama, coming and going*. New York: Greenwillow Books.
    A mother juggles many responsibilities
Child, L. (2005). *Hubert Horatio Bartle Bobton Trent*. New York: Hyperion.
    A boy prodigy and his parents, living in wealth, learn to value closeness when
    their money is gone
Cowen-Fletcher, J. (1993). *Mama zooms*. New York: Scholastic.
    A mother uses a wheelchair to "zoom" with her child on various adventures

Davol, M. W. (1993). *Black, white, just right*. Morton Grove, IL: Albert Whitman.
    A biracial child describes her uniqueness
Galloway, P. (1985). *Jennifer has two daddies*. Toronto: Women's Press.
    A girl lives with her mom and stepfather one week and with her dad the next,
    and has a relationship with both fathers
Garden N. (2004). *Molly's family*. New York: Farrar, Strauss and Giroux.
    Molly, who has two mommies, realizes that her friends' families are not the
    same as hers
Geheret, J. (1990). *The don't-give-up kid and learning differences*. Fairport, NY: Verbal Images Press.
    Alex learns others have learning differences
Gellman, E. (1992). *Jeremy's dreidel*. Rockville, MD: Kar-Ben Copies.
    A Jewish child learns about family rituals and his grandparent's blindness
Heelan, J. R., & Simmonds, N. (2002). *Can you hear a rainbow?* Atlanta, GA: Peachtree.
    A picture of the strengths of children with different abilities
Hoffman, A. (2000). *Horsefly*. New York: Hyperion Books for Children.
    A girl transcends fears
Horowitz, R. (1991). *Bat time*. New York: Four Winds Press, Macmillan.
    A girl and her father go looking for bats
Janus Kahn, K. (1989). *Alef is one: A Hebrew alphabet counting book*. Rockville, MD: Kar-Ben Copies.
    Hebrew letters introduce counting concepts
Juster, N. (2005). *The hello, goodbye window*. New York: Michael Di Capua Books.
    The loving relationship between interracial grandparents and their
    grandchild
Kitze, C. (2003) *I don't have your eyes*. EMK.
    Transracial and transcultural adoption
Lester, H. (1999). *Hooway for Wodney Wat*. New York: Scholastic.
    Withstanding speech challenges, shyness, teasing, and bullying
Lifton, B. J. (1993). *Tell me a real adoption story*. New York: Alfred A. Knopf.
    Adopted child, birth and adoptive parent
Lindsay, J. W. (1999). *Do I have a Daddy?* Buena Park, CA: Morning Glory Press.
    About a single-parent family
Litchfield, A. (1980). *Words in our hands*. Chicago: Albert Whitman.
    A hearing child lives with deaf parents
MacLachlan, P. (1987). *Mama one, Mama two*. New York: HarperCollins.
    Foster child deals with loss and grief
Martin, B. (1997). *SWISH*. New York: Henry Holt.
    Girls play basketball
McCourt, L. (1998). *The braids girl*. Deerfield Beach, FL: Health Communications.
    Two children meet at a homeless shelter and develop an understanding of
    friendship
McCully, E. (1989). *Friday night is Papa night*. New York: Puffin Books.
    A father comes home every Friday night from his out-of-town job

Millman, I. (1998). *Moses goes to a concert*. New York: Frances, Straus and Giroux.
   American Sign Language demonstrated in story about a deaf boy
Mills, L. (1991). *The rag coat*. New York: Little Brown.
   Minna's classmates make fun of her new winter coat, made with scraps of
   quilting material
Parr, T. (2001). *It's okay to Be different*. New York: Little Brown.
   Different families, different abilities, competition, and friendship
Pinkwater, D. M. (1977). *The big orange splot*. New York: Scholastic.
   Making your own mark and appreciating uniqueness
Quinlan, P. (1987). *My dad takes care of me*. Toronto: Annick Press.
   Changes in a family because of unemployment
Ransom, C. (1993). *We're growing together*. New York: Bradbury Press.
   Family changes when a parent remarries
Raschka, C. (1990). *R and Я: A Story about two alphabets*. Elgin, IL: Brethren Press.
   English and Russian alphabet letters discover similarities and an end to
   conflict
Reid, R. (2002). *The big storm*. New York: Scholastic.
   Family members help little Bill solve the problem of his fears
Rosenberg, L. (1995). *The carousel*. New York: Harcourt Brace.
   Two sisters remember their mother, who "could fix anything"
Senisi, E. B. (1998). *For my family, love, Allie*. Morton Grove, IL: Albert Whitman.
   Allie struggles to give a gift to her extended, biracial family
Skutch, R. (1998). *Who's in a family?* Berkeley, CA: Tricycle Press.
   Many kinds of white families
Smalls, I. (2000). *Kevin and his dad*. New York: Scholastic.
   Father and son do everyday tasks that counter gender stereotypes
Spinelli, E. (2000). *Night Shift Daddy*. New York: Hyperion Books.
   A father works at night.
Wickens, E. (1994). *Anna Day and the O-ring*. Boston: Alyson Wonderland.
   Four-year-old searches for a missing piece of his new tent, with help from
   his two moms
Williams, V. (1984). *A chair for my mother*. New York: Harper Trophy
   A daughter's gift of love to her working-class, single mom.
Zolotow, C. (1972) *William's doll*. New York: HarperCollins.
   One of the first books to challenge gender stereotyping
Zucker, D. (1993). *Uncle Carmello*. New York: Simon & Schuster.
   Breaking down language barriers in a white family

DIVERSITY BEYOND FAMILY AND IMMEDIATE NEIGHBORHOOD

Ada, A. F. (2002). *Gathering the sun*. New York: Harper Collins.
   Poems about working migrant children and pride in one's language
Ajmera, M., & Ivanko, J. D. (1999). *To be a kid*. Watertown, MA: Charlesbridge.
   Similarities among children all over the world

Alshalabi, F. M. (1995). *Ahmed's alphabet*. Washington, DC: American Educational Trust (for Rubeian Publishing). (See AET in Appendix B.).

  Ahmed introduces himself, his family, culture, and background

Argueta, J. (2003). *Xochitl and the flowers/Xóchitl, la niña de las flores*. San Francisco: Children's Book Press.

  A family transforms a garbage heap into a plant nursery

Ashley, B. (1991). *Cleversticks*. New York: Crown.

  Children teach and learn from one another

Choi, Y. (2001). *The name jar*. New York: Knopf Books for Young Readers.

  Unhei worries that she will be teased about her Korean name

Dorros, A. (1992). *This is my house*. New York: Scholastic.

  Drawings of many kinds of houses

Fowler, C. (1998). *Shota and the Star Quilt*. New York: Zero to Ten Limited.

  In English and Lakota, about a current Native American family and their traditions

Garland, S. (2002). *My father's boat*. New York: Scholastic.

  Vietnamese father passes family stories to his son while working together on a shrimp boat

Heide, F. P,. & Gilliland, J. H. (1995). *The day of Ahmed's secret*. New York: Lothrop, William Morrow

  In Lebanon, Ahmed waits to tell his family his secret: He can write his name

Herrera, J. (2001). *Calling the doves/El canto de las palomas*. San Francisco: Children's Book Press.

  A child recalls growing up with Mexican American farmworker parents

Herrera J., Rohmer, H., Cumpiano, I., & De Lucio-Brock, A. (2002). *Grandma and me at the flea/Los meros meros remateros*. San Francisco: Children's Book Press.

  Young Juanito and his grandmother sell old clothes at a flea market

Hoffman, M. (1991). *Amazing Grace*. New York: Dial Books.

  An African American girl stands up against gender and race bias, supported by her family

Igus, T. (2001). *Two Mrs. Gibson's*. San Francisco: Children's Book Press.

  The blending of Japanese and African American culture, identity, and family

Johnson-Davis, D. (1995). *Animal tales from the Arab world*. Cairo, Egypt: Hoopoe Books. (See American Educational Trust (AET) in Appendix B.)

  Tales adapted from traditional Arabic fables about wise, foolish, and proud animals

Joose, B. M. (1991). *Mama, do you love me?* San Francisco: Chronicle Books.

  An Inuit mother and daughter have a dialogue about unconditional love

Keeshig-Tobias, L. (1993). *Bird talk*. Toronto: Sister Vision, Black Women & Women of Colour Press.

  A First Nation child handles stereotyping about her identity, with support from her mother

Kissinger, K. (1994). *All the colors we are/Todos los colores de nuestra piel: The story of how we get our skin color/La historia de por que tenemos diferentes colores de piel*. St. Paul, MN: Redleaf Press.

  Clearly explains how we get our skin color

Martin, B., & Archambault, J. (1987). *Knots on a counting rope.* New York: Henry Holt.
> A blind child hears the story of his birth and childhood in his Navajo community from his grandfather

Monk, I. (2001). *Family.* New York: Scholastic.
> An African American family going on a trip to Aunt Poogee's farm for a reunion

Nye, S. N. (1994). *Sitti's secrets.* New York: Simon & Schuster Books for Young Children.
> An Arab American girl travels to the Middle East to meet her Palestinian grandmother

Pérez, A. (2000). *My very own room/Mi propio cuarito.* San Francisco: Children's Book Press.
> A large, loving Latino family works together to make a young girl's dream come true

Profilet, C. (1990). *Kamal's quest.* Ridgeland, MS: Sterling Press.
> A young camel, who has lost his mother, is befriended by kind Arabs in Bahrain.

Rattigan, J. (1993). *Dumpling soup.* New York: Little Brown.
> Celebrates customs and languages of many cultures

Ringgold, F. (1996). *Bonjour Lonnie.* New York: Hyperion Books for Children.
> Mixed heritage, weaving of African American experience

Schwalm, C. (1998). *Being bilingual is fun.* Alameda, CA: Cultural Connections.
> The joys and benefits of being bilingual

Simon, N., & Flavin, T. (2003). *All families are special.* Morton Grove, IL: Albert Whitman.
> Kindergarten children tell about their families

Williams, S. A. (1997). *Working cotton.* New York: Harcourt Brace.
> A young African American girl's life as a migrant farm worker

Yamate, S. (1991). *Char Siu Bao Boy.* Chicago: Polychrome.
> Charlie, Chinese American, learns to appreciate himself despite pressure from his peers

CONNECTION, COOPERATION, AND CHALLENGING PREJUDICE

Anzaldúa, G. (1993). *Friends from the other side/Amigos del otro lado.* San Francisco: Children's Book Press.
> Faced with prejudice from his peers, Joaquin receives help from his friend

Bunnett, R. (1995). *Friends at school.* New York: Scholastic.
> Sharing, support, and learning from one another across diversity

Escudie, R. (1988). *Paul and Sebastian.* New York: Kane Miller Books.
> Two boys become friends despite their mothers' disapproval of the other's living situation

Fleming, V. (1993). *Be good to Eddie Lee.* New York: Philomel Books.
> Eddie Lee, a child with Down's syndrome, and Christy become friends

Fujimoto, M. (1996). *Go team!* New York: Putnam.
Countering stereotypical gender roles to work together
Fujimoto, M. (1996). *I can't sleep.* New York: Putnam.
Using cooperation to accommodate different habits and routines
Hooks, G. (2004). *Three's a crowd.* New York: Scholastic.
Learning friendship skills across cultural differences.
Lester, J. (2005). *Let's talk about race.* New York: HarperCollins.
A discussion about racism for school-age children
Lipniacka, E. (2003). *Who shares?* New York: Dial Books for Young Readers.
Explores issues in learning to share
Lyon, G. E. (1989). *Together.* New York: Scholastic.
The power of the friendship between two girls from different cultural
backgrounds
Merrifield, M. (1998). *Come sit by me.* Toronto: Women's Press.
When other children reject Nicholas, who has AIDS, Karen reaches out to him
Newman, L. (1991). *Belinda's bouquet.* Boston: Alyson Wonderland.
A girl with two moms helps a friend who is teased about being fat
Polacco, P. (1992). *Chicken Sunday.* New York: Philomel Books.
A white child's relationship with an African American family
Polacco, P. (1992). *Mrs. Katz and Tush.* New York: Bantam Little Rooster.
A young African American boy befriends an elderly Jewish woman
Reiser, L. (1996). *Margaret and Margarita.* New York: Mulberry Books.
Two girls meet in the park and communicate bilingually
Rosen, M. (1996). *This is our house.* Cambridge, MA: Candlewick Press.
George, who excludes classmates, finds out how it feels to be excluded
Seskin, S., & Shamblin, A. (2002). *Don't laugh at me.* Berkeley, CA: Tricycle Press.
Bullied and teased children find their voice
Thomas, P. (2003). *Is it right to fight?* New York: Barron's Educational.
Explores anger and ways to deal with disagreements
Verdick, E. (2004). *Words are not for hurting.* Minneapolis, MN: Free Spirit.
Explores the power of words
Wildsmith, B. (1992). *The owl and the woodpecker.* New York: Oxford University Press.
Other animals help resolve a dispute between a woodpecker and an owl

CARING FOR AND SHARING THE RESOURCES OF THE EARTH

Base, G. (2001) *The waterhole.* New York: Harry N. Abrams.
Animals watch the waterhole disappear over time
Cherry, L. (1990). *The great kapok tree.* San Diego, CA: Harcourt, Brace, Jovanovich.
Together, the living beings of a rain forest—human and animal—persuade
a man to stop cutting down the trees
Dr. Seuss. (1971). *The Lorax.* New York: Random House.
Activism strategies in the face of pollution and other negative consequences
of manufacturing

Flourney, V. (1985). *The patchwork quilt*. New York: Dial Books for Young Children.
> African American family recycles material resources and learns about their heritage

Griese, A. (1995). *Anna's Athbaskan summer*. Honesdale, PA: Boyds Mills Press.
> Native Athbaskans use natural resources without harming the earth

Hoyt-Goldsmith, D. (1993). *Cherokee summer*. New York: Holiday House.
> A Cherokee girl's family preserves unity with the natural environment by blending tradition with current life

Humphrey, M. (1987). *The river that gave gifts*. San Francisco: Children's Book Press.
> Three African American sisters, working together, show that the best presents are made with love

Karas, G. (2005). *On earth*. New York: G. P. Putnam Sons.
> Sharing the planet

Levine, A. A. (1993). *Pearl Moscowitz's last stand*. New York: Tambourine Books.
> An elderly Jewish woman and her neighbors save the last ginkgo tree in their diverse urban neighborhood

Nikola-Lisa, W. (2002). *Summer sun risin'*. New York: Lee & Low Books.
> African American family works together through a day on their farm

Radunsky, V. (2004). *What does peace feel like?* New York: Anne Schwartz Books.
> Children around the world describe peace

Raffi (1996). *Everything grows* [recording]. Cambridge, MA: Rounder.
> Songs about how everything grows and changes

Rascal (1994). *Oregon's journey*. Mahwah, NJ: BridgeWater Books.
> A little person helps a circus bear escape to freedom

Shelby, A. (1993). *What to do about pollution*. New York: Orchard Books.
> About pollution, its consequences, and possible solutions

WORKING FOR FAIRNESS AND SOCIAL CHANGE

Cohn, D. (2002). *Si, se puede! Yes, we can*. El Paso, TX: Cinco Puntos Press.
> Bilingual story about the successful Justice for Janitors strike in Los Angeles, told through the eyes of a young boy

Coles, R. (1995). *The story of Ruby Bridges*. New York: Scholastic.
> True story about the first African American child to attend a southern all-white elementary school

Cronin, D. (2000). *Click clack moo—Cows that type*. New York: Simon & Schuster.
> Cows and chickens on a farm strike for better conditions

DiSalvo-Ryan, D. (1991). *Uncle Willie and the soup kitchen*. New York: Morrow.
> A young boy helps his uncle, who volunteers in a soup kitchen

Farris, C. (2003). *My brother Martin*. New York: Simon & Schuster.
> Remembering growing up with the Reverend Dr. Martin Luther King Jr.

Golenbock, P. (1990). *Teammates*. New York: Harcourt Brace.
> Jackie Robinson deals with prejudice with help from a white teammate

Greenfield, E. (1973). *Rosa Parks*. New York: Harper.

>Rosa Parks and the Montgomery Bus Boycott

Guthrie, D. (1988). *A rose for Abby*. Nashville: Abingdon Press.

>Seeing a homeless woman searching the trash cans for food, Abby takes action

Hoffman, E. (1999). *No fair to tigers/No es justo para los tigres*. St. Paul, MN: Redleaf Press.

>A girl with a disability insists on fair treatment

Hoffman, E. (1999). *Play lady/La señora juguetona*. St. Paul, MN: Redleaf Press.

>Children come to the aid of a neighbor when she is the target of a hate crime

Kivel, P. (2001). *I can make my world a safer place: A Kid's book about stopping violence*. Alameda, CA: Hunter House.

>Social justice activities for school-age children

Krull, K. (2003). *Harvesting hope*. New York: Harcourt Children's Books.

>The story of labor and social justice activist Caesar Chavez

Kurusa. (1995). *The streets are free*. Buffalo, NY: Annick Press.

>Children get parents and neighbors involved in a campaign for a city park

Lionni, L. (1963). *Swimmy*. New York: Alfred A. Knopf.

>How a school of small fish stand up to a big fish who threatens their survival

Perez, L. K. (2002). *First day in grapes*. New York: Lee and Low Books.

>Growing up in a migrant family and standing up for yourself

Rappaport, D. (2001). *Martin's big words*. New York: Jump at the Sun Hyperion Books.

>Powerful statements about social justice and activism from Rev. Martin Luther King Jr.

Ringgold, F. (1995). *My dream of Martin Luther King*. New York: Crown.

>Rev. Martin Luther King Jr. and the civil rights movement described for young children

Wiles, D. (2001). *Freedom Summer. New York:* Atheneum Books.

>An interracial friendship and the impact of the civil rights movement in a Southern town

Winter, J. & J. (1991). *Diego*. New York: Alfred Knopf.

>Story of the activist artist, who painted the history and life of the Mexican working people; in English and Spanish

Wood, T., with Wanbli Numpa Afraid of Hawk. (1992). *A boy becomes a man at Wounded Knee*. New York: Walker.

>A Native American boy retraces his ancestral roots and learns to face challenges

CURRICULUM RESOURCES

Early Childhood

Bisson, J. (1997). *Celebrate! An anti-bias guide to enjoying holidays in early childhood programs*. St. Paul, MN: Redleaf Press.

Brown, B. (2001). *Combating discrimination: Persona dolls in action.* London: Trentham Books.

Copple, C. (Ed.). (2003). *A world of difference: Readings on teaching young children in a diverse society.* Washington, DC: National Association for the Education of Young Children.

Derman-Sparks, L., & the A.B.C. Task Force. (1989). *Anti-bias curriculum: Tools for empowering young children.* Washington, DC: National Association for the Education of Young Children.

Hoffman, E. (2005). *Magic capes, amazing powers: Transforming superhero play in the classroom.* St. Paul, MN: Redleaf Press.

Pelo, A., & Davidson, F. (2000). *That's not fair! A teacher's guide to activism with young children.* St. Paul, MN: Redleaf Press.

Ramsey, P. G. (2004). *Teaching and learning in a diverse world: Multicultural education for young children* (3rd. ed.). New York: Teachers College Press.

Whitney, T. (1999). *Kids like us: Using persona dolls in the classroom.* St. Paul, MN: Redleaf Press.

Wolpert, E. (1999). *Start seeing diversity: The basic guide to an anti-bias classroom* [Video and guide]. St. Paul, MN: Redleaf Press.

York, S. (2003). *Big as life: The everyday inclusive curriculum* (Vols. 1 & 2). St. Paul, MN: Redleaf Press.

Primary/Upper Primary School

Bigelow, B. (Ed.). (1994, 2001). *Rethinking our classrooms: Teaching for equity and justice* (Vols. 1 & 2). Milwaukee, WI: Rethinking Schools.

Lee, E., Menkart, D., & Okazawa-Rey, M. (2002). *Beyond heroes and holidays.* Washington, DC: Teaching for Change.

Sapon-Shevin, M. (1999). *Because we can change the world: A practical guide to building cooperative, inclusive classroom communities.* New York: Allyn & Bacon.

Schniedewind, N., & Davidson, E. (1998). *Open minds to equality: A source book of learning activities to affirm diversity and promote equity.* New York: Allyn and Bacon.

Organizations and Web Sites

Lack of information is no longer an obstacle to doing anti-bias/ multicultural education and activism work. The following list offers a range of organizational and Web site resources. Each listing leads to additional sites. Please exercise critical thinking about any material you choose to use in your work.

AET Book Club, *www.middleeastbooks.com:* Children and adult books, videos, and CD Roms about Arab-Americans and people living in the Middle East.

American Arab Anti-Discrimination Committee, *www.adc.org*: Material for supporting Arab American children and families and for teaching about Arab Americans with all children.

American Friends Service Committee, *www.afsc.org*: Programs related to economic justice, peace-building and demilitarization, social justice, and youth in the United States and in Africa, Asia, Latin America, and the Middle East.

Applied Research Center, *www.arc.org*: A public-policy, educational, and research institute working on issues of race, racism, and social change in schools and in health-related and other institutions.

California Tomorrow, *www.californiatomorrow.org*: Action research and resources for working with adults and children on issues of culture, language, immigration, and equity in schools.

Center for New Community, *www.newcomm.org*: Education and community organizing for immigrants rights, anti-racism, and other social-justice issues in rural areas and small cities.

Center for the Study of White American Culture, *www.euroamerican.org*: Resources and opportunities for discussions about the multifaceted issues of whiteness.

Children's Books Press, *www.childrensbookpress.net*: Bilingual books about a range of children and families of color.

Civil Rights Coalition for the 21st Century, *www.civilrights.org*: Web site of the Leadership Conference on Civil Rights and links to several other national organizations working on a range of civil rights issues.

Civil Rights Teaching, *www.civilrightsteaching.org*: Information to use with adults and to adapt for children.

Cooperative Children's Book Center, *www.education.wisc.edu/ccbc*: Bibliographies of children's books on a variety of diversity issues.

Crossroads Ministry, *www.crossraodsministry.org*: Anti-racism work in faith-based and educational institutions. Resources for furthering learning about racism.

Donnelly Colt, *www.donnellycolt.com*: Social-justice posters, bumper stickers, buttons, T-shirts.

Educational Equity Concepts, Inc., *www.edequity.org*: Preschool-to-third-grade resources for addressing equity issues related to disability, gender, and bullying, with further Web links on each topic.

Educators for Social Responsibility, *www.esrnational.org*: Resources on conflict resolution, violence prevention, and character education.

Gay, Lesbian, and Straight Education Network, *www.glsen.org*: Resources and information to assure equity in relation to sexual orientation and gender identity/expression.

Gustavus Myers Center for the Study of Bigotry and Human Rights, *www.myerscenter.org*: Reviews of new books and videos for adults and children.

Independent Living USA, *www.ilusa.com*: Information, news, resources, and numerous links for all issues related to children, adults, and families with disabilities.

National Association of Multicultural Education, *www.nameorg.org*: Annual conference, journal, and a Listserv. Good place to stay current on a range of diversity and equity educational work.

Poverty and Race Research Action Council, *www.prrac.org*: Generates and disseminates research on the relationship between race and poverty and promotes policies and practices for local, state, and national advocacy groups.

Rethinking Schools, *www.rethinkingschools.org*: Excellent journal on a range of equity issues related to education. Curriculum ideas for working with elementary and high school students.

Social Justice Resources Center, *http://http.//edpsychserver.ed.vt.edu/diversity*: Searchable databases with numerous print, media, and Web-based resources relevant to developing diversity-inclusive curricula and pedagogy for students, faculty, and educators in K–12 and higher education.

Syracuse Cultural Workers, *www.syrculturalworkers.com*: Social-justice posters, bumper stickers, and pins.

Teaching for Change, *www.teaching forchange.org*: Outstanding books, videos, and posters for educators in preschool, primary, secondary, and higher education; excellent links to a range of additional Web sites. A great place to begin.

Tim Wise Home Page, *www.TimeWise.org*: Enlightening essays about current issues facing white anti-racist activists.

Voices of Civil Rights, *www.voicesofcivilright.org*: Personal accounts of Americans struggling to fulfill the promise of equality for all. Project of the AARP, Leadership Conference on Civil Rights (LCCR), and Library of Congress.

Selected White Anti-racism Activists in the 20th and 21st Centuries

COMPILED BY BILL SPARKS

Name	Description	Period of Work	Reference
Adams, Emmie Shrader	Growing up in Minnesota, she worked in northern Mississippi to encourage poor white farmers to fight for their rights with black farmers. On staff of SNCC.	1961–1965	Curry et al., 2002
Barndt, Joseph	Founder of Crossroads Ministry, a faith-based community that does anti-racism education and organizing among Christian congregations.	1960–present	*www.cross roadsministry. org*
Braden, Anne, and Carl	Pioneering and inspirational leaders against racist southern practices, including organizing white and interracial groups to educate others. Helped to found the Southern Organizing Committee.	1955–present	C. S. Brown, 2002
Burlage, Dorothy Dawson	Dorothy's call to the mostly white National Student Association influenced their vote to support the civil rights movement. She organized in Texas for school desegregation, church activism, and voter registration.	1955–1970	Curry et al., 2002
Campbell, Will D.	Challenged southern churches and Christians to support the ending of segregation and to establish civil rights for all. Organized interracial dialogue groups. Considered a "Spiritual Mentor" to the whites in the Freedom Movement (civil rights movement).	1950–1965	Curry et al., 2002

(*continued*)

Name	Description	Period of Work	Reference
Curry, Constance	Active in the South before the first sit-ins, she helped organize the first Student Non-violent Coordinating Committee (SNCC) office. She pioneered effective strategies to work with white churches, student organizations, and white women's groups to promote school desegregation in the south.	1958–1966	Curry et al., 2002
Dees, Morris	Co-founder of the Southern Poverty Law Center (with Joseph Levin, Jr. and Julian Bond in 1971), Morris Dees has been its chief trial lawyer and conceptual leader. The Southern Poverty Law Center has legally and successfully fought several white-supremacist hate organizations and publishes anti-racial prejudice resources for educators at all levels, including its magazine *Teaching for Tolerance*.	1970–present	M. Dees, 2001 *www.SPL Center.org*
Del Pozzo, Theresa	She helped found the Northern Student Movement, an anti-racist group that was active against northern racism and raised funds for SNCC and others.	1955–1970	Curry et al., 2002
Durr, Virginia Foster	Invoked the Christian themes of honesty and integrity to challenge everyday racism in southern life.	1940–1950	C. S. Brown, 2002
Gunderson, Margaret; Smeltzer, Mary; Ferguson, Lois and Charles—and 190 others	White teachers who taught school in the Japanese-American Internment Camps set up in the United States during World War II. They faced army and community hostility.	1940–1945	L.A. Times, 2/5/05, p. B1
Goodman, Andrew	Along with James Chaney (African American) and Michael Schwerner, left northern colleges for Mississippi Summer voting rights drive in 1964. Murdered by Ku Klux Klan.	1960–1964	R. Takaki, 1993
Greenberg, Jack	Head of the NAACP Legal Defense and Education Fund	1947–1963	R. Takaki, 1993

Name	Description	Period of Work	Reference
Hayden, Casey	She helped prepare the delegation of the Mississippi Freedom Democratic Party (MFDP) at the 1964 Democratic Convention by having committees in every Mississippi county. Later she worked in Atlanta city programs when Andrew Young was mayor.	1961–1990	Curry et al., 2002
Hill, Herbert	Director of NAACP's labor drives in the South.	1949–1954	R. Takaki, 1993
Horton, Myles	Founder of the pioneering Highlander Center in Tennessee, which does anti-racist, labor, and environmental-justice education and organizing in the South. Among many others, Rosa Parks studied at Highlander.	1940–1990	Horton et al., 1998
Kohl, Herb R.	Educational innovator, teacher, and writer about racism and anti-racism in education.	1962–present	C. S. Brown, 2002
Liuzzo, Viola Gregg	Previously not an activist, she decided to drive to Montgomery, Alabama, to help with the Selma-to-Montgomery March and provide transportation to the marchers in her old station wagon. She was murdered by the Klu Klux Klan.	1962	C. S. Brown, 2002
Mathews, John Prentice and John Prentice Jr	Father-and-son residents of small Mississippi towns who formed multiracial organizations to fight for the rights of African Americans. Were assassinated by opponents.	1865–1922	C. S. Brown, 2002
Olsen, Laurie	Cofounder and executive director of California Tomorrow, an anti-racism action research organization that produces outstanding resources for combating racism in schools and for implementing culturally relevant and bilingual education for children.	1985–present	*ww.california tomorrow.org*
Schwerner, Michael	*See* Goodman, Andrew		
Thrasher, Sue	Active in the Student United Nations and the Methodist Student Union, she helped start the Southern Strategy Organizing Committee, a group of white activists. She was the first archivist at Highlander Center.	1962–1989	Curry et al, 2002

(continued)

Name	Description	Period of Work	Reference
Wallace, Beth	Editor of several books for adults and children on anti-bias/anti-racism education in early childhood programs.	1985– present	Alvarado et al., 1999
Wilkinson, Frank	Pioneer in creating public housing in Los Angeles and elsewhere, and fought from the beginning for integrated housing. Also worked in several multiracial coalitions to end segregation in all aspects of public life.	1950– 1980	C. S. Brown, 2002
Zinn, Howard	Historian and author about anti-racist social-justice movements, current and historical. His best known book, *The People's History of the United States*, has sold 400,000 copies.	1960– present	Zinn, 1995

What Do Trees Have to Do with Peace?

DENISE ROY

Thirty years ago, in the country of Kenya, 90% of the forest had been chopped down. Without trees to hold the topsoil in place, the land became like a desert. When the women and girls would go in search of firewood in order to prepare the meals, they would have to spend hours and hours looking for what few branches remained.

A woman named Wangari watched all of this happening. She decided that there must be a way to take better care of the land and take better care of the women and girls. So she planted a tree. And then she planted another.

She wanted to plant thousands of trees, but she realized that it would take a very long time if she was the only one doing it. So she taught the women who were looking for firewood to plant trees, and they were paid a small amount for each sapling they grew.

Soon she organized women all over the country to plant trees, and a movement took hold. It was called the Green Belt Movement. With each passing year, more and more trees covered the land. But something else was happening as the women planted those trees. Something else besides those trees was taking root. The women began to have confidence in themselves. They began to see that they could make a difference. They began to see that they were capable of many things and that they were equal to the men. They began to recognize that they were deserving of being treated with respect and dignity.

Changes like these were threatening to some. The president of the country didn't like any of this. So police were sent to intimidate and beat Wangari for planting trees, and for planting ideas of equality and democracy in people's heads, especially in women's. She was accused of "subversion" and arrested many times. Once, while Wangari was trying to plant trees, she was clubbed by guards hired by developers who wanted the lands cleared. She was hospitalized with head injuries. But she survived, and it only made her realize that she was on the right path.

For almost 30 years, she was threatened physically, and she was often made fun of in the press. But she didn't flinch. She only had to look in the eyes of her three children, and in the eyes of the thousands of women and girls who were blossoming right along with the trees, and she found the strength to continue.

And that is how it came to be that 30 million trees have been planted in Africa, one tree at a time. The landscapes—both the external one of the land and the internal one of the people—have been transformed.

In 2002, the people of Kenya held a democratic election, and the president who opposed Wangari and her Green Belt Movement is no longer in office. And Wangari became Kenya's Assistant Minister for the Environment. After her appointment to the government, she told the U.N. Environmental Programme:

> Our recent experience in Kenya gives hope to all who have been struggling for a better future. It shows it is possible to bring about positive change, and still do it peacefully. All it takes is courage and perseverance, and a belief that positive change is possible. That is why the slogan for our campaign was "Yote Yaawezekana!" or "It is possible!"

She is 65 years old, and in 2004 she planted one more tree in celebration and thanksgiving for being given a very great honor: Wangari Maathai has been awarded the Nobel Peace Prize. She is the first African woman to receive this award. After she was notified, she gave a speech entitled, "What Do Trees Have to Do with Peace?" She pointed out how most wars are fought over limited natural resources, such as oil, land, or diamonds. She called for an end to corporate greed, and for leaders to build more just societies. She added:

> On behalf of all African women, I want to express my profound appreciation for this honour, which will serve to encourage women in Kenya, in Africa, and around the world to raise their voices and not to be deterred. When we plant trees, we plant the seeds of peace and seeds of hope. We also secure the future for our children.
>
> One of the first things I did yesterday when I got the extraordinary news about this prize was to plant a Nandi flame tree. . . . So, on this wonderful occasion, I call on Kenyans and those around the world to celebrate by planting a tree wherever you are.

As she received the Nobel Peace Prize in Oslo, she invited us all to get involved:

> Today we are faced with a challenge that calls for a shift in our thinking, so that humanity stops threatening its life-support system. We are called to assist the Earth to heal her wounds and in the process heal our own—indeed, to embrace the whole creation in all its diversity, beauty and wonder. This will happen if we see the need to revive our sense of belonging to a larger family of life.

Reflection Questions

- Can we accept Wangari's invitation?
- As we look around our neighborhood or city, as we look at our own country, what is needed?
- Where are women and children suffering?
- Where are people feeling disempowered?
- Where does the Earth need our help?
- What is our equivalent of planting one tree?

References

Aboud, F. E., & Doyle, A. B. (1995). The development of in-group pride in Black Canadians. *Journal of Cross Cultural Psychology, 26*(3), 243–254.

Aboud, F. E., & Doyle, A. B. (1996a). Does talk of race foster prejudice or tolerance in children? *Canadian Journal of Behavioural Science, 28*(3), 161–170.

Aboud, F. E., & Doyle, A. B. (1996b). Parental and peer influences on children's racial attitudes. *International Journal of Intercultural Relations, 20*(3/4), 371 383.

Allen, Theodore W. (1994). *The invention of the white race: Racial oppression and social control* (Vol. 1). London: Verso.

Alvarado, C., Derman-Sparks, L., & Ramsey, P. G. (1999). *In our own way: How anti-bias work shapes our lives.* St. Paul, MN: Redleaf Press.

Aptheker, H. (1993). *Anti-racism in U.S. history: The first 200 years.* Westport, CT: Praeger.

Barndt, J. (1991). *Dismantling racism: The continuing challenge to white America.* Minneapolis, MN: Augsburg.

Barndt, J., & Ruehle, C. (1992). Rediscovering a heritage lost: A European-American anti-racist identity. In *America's original sin: A study guide on white racism* (Rev. ed.; pp. 73–77). Washington, DC: Sojourners Resource Center.

Barrett, J. R., & Roediger, D. (2002). How white people became white. In P. S. Rothenberg (Ed.), *White privilege: Essential readings on the other side of racism* (pp. 29–34). New York: Worth.

Bigler, R. S., Jones, L. C., & Lobliner, D. B. (1997). Social categorization and the formation of intergroup attitudes in children. *Child Development, 68*(3), 530–543.

Bigler, R. S., & Liben, L. S. (1993). A cognitive-developmental approach to racial stereotyping and reconstructive memory in Euro-American children. *Child Development, 64*, 1507–1518.

Bisson, J. (1997). *Celebrate! An anti-bias guide to enjoying holidays in early childhood programs.* St. Paul, MN: Redleaf Press.

Bonze, J. (1998, July). Words that smear, like 'racism,' provoke polarization. *San Francisco Chronicle*, p. D7.

Brady, P. (1996, April). The journey towards anti-racist identity for multi-racial people, people of color & whites. *The Web*, p. 9. (Out of print)

Brodkin, K. (1998). *How Jews became white folks and what that says about race in America.* New Brunswick, NJ: Rutgers University Press.

Brodkin, K. (2002). How Jews became white folks. In P. S. Rothenberg (Ed.), *White privilege: Essential readings on the other side of racism* (pp. 35–48). (New York: Worth.

Brown, B. (1998). *Unlearning discrimination in the early years*. London: Trentham Books.

Brown, B. (2001). *Combating discrimination: Persona dolls in action*. London: Trentham Books.

Brown, C. S. (2002). *Refusing racism: White allies and the struggle for civil rights*. New York: Teachers College Press.

Brown, N. (1998, August). *The impact of culture on the education of young children with special needs*. Paper presented at the biennial meeting of the Organization Mondiale de l'Education Preescolaire, Copenhagen, Denmark.

Browser, B., & Hunt, R. (1981). *Impacts of racism on white Americans*. Beverly Hills, CA: Sage.

Burnett, M. N., & Sisson, K. (1995). Doll studies revisited: A question of validity. *Journal of Black Psychology, 21*(1), 19–29.

Bush, M. E. L. (2004). *Breaking the code of good intentions: Everyday forms of whiteness*. New York: Rowan & Littlefield.

Cadwell, L. B. (2003). *Bringing learning to life: The Reggio approach to early childhood education*. New York: Teachers College Press.

Carter, M., & Curtis, D. (1997). *Training teachers: A harvest of theory and practice*. St. Paul, MN: Redleaf Press.

Chafel, J. A. (1997). Children's views of poverty: A review of research and implications for teaching. *The Educational Forum, 61*, 360–371.

Chang, H. N.-L., Femeneall, T., Louise, N., Murdock B., & Pell, E. (2000). *Walking the walk: Principles for building community capacity for equity and diversity*. Oakland, CA: California Tomorrow.

Chang, H. N.-L., Muckelroy, A., & Pulido-Tobiassen, D. (1996). *Looking in, looking out: Redefining child care and early education in a diverse society*. Oakland, CA: California Tomorrow.

Chennault, R. E. (1998). Giving whiteness a black eye: An interview with Michael Erik Dyson. In J. L. Kincheloe, S. R. Steinberg, N. M. Rodriguez, & R. E. Chennault (Eds.), *White reign: Deploying whiteness in America* (pp. 299–328). New York: St. Martin's Griffin.

Cherry, L. (1990). *The great kapok tree*. New York: Harcourt Brace Jovanovich.

Children's Defense Fund. (2005). *The state of America's children*. Washington, DC: Author.

Clark, K. B. (1963). *Prejudice and your child*. Boston: Beacon Press.

Clark, K. B., & Clark, M. P. (1947). Racial identification and preference in Negro children. In T. M. Newcomb & E. L. Hartley (Eds.), *Readings in social psychology* (pp. 169–178). New York: Free Press.

Colby, A., & Damon, W. (1992). *Some do care: Contemporary lives of moral commitment*. New York: Free Press.

Coles, R. (1977). *Privileged ones: The well-off and the rich in America*. Boston: Little, Brown.

Cronin, S., Derman-Sparks, L., Henry, S., Olatunji, C., & York, S. (1998). *Future vision, present work: Learning from the Culturally Relevant Anti-Bias Leadership Project*. St. Paul, MN: Redleaf.

Cross, W. E., Jr. (1985). Black identity: Rediscovering the distinction between personal identity and reference group orientation. In M. B. Spencer, G. K. Brookins, & W. R. Allen (Eds.), *Beginnings: The social and affective development of black children* (pp. 155–171). Hillsdale, NJ: Lawrence Erlbaum Associates.

Cross, W. E., Jr. (1991). *Shades of black: Diversity in African-American identity*. Philadelphia: Temple University Press.

Curry, C., et al. (2000). *Deep in our hearts: Nine white women in the freedom movement*. Athens: University of Georgia Press.

Damon, W. (1980). Patterns of change in children's social reasoning: A 2-year longitudinal study. *Child Development, 51*, 1010–1017.

Davis, A. (1983). *Women, race, and class*. New York: Vintage.

Dees, M. (2001). *A lawyer's journey: The Morris Dees story*. Washington, DC: American Bar Association.

Delpit, L., & Dowdy, J. (Eds.). (2002). *The skin that we speak*. New York: New Press.

Derman-Sparks, L., & A.B.C. Task Force. (1989). *Anti-bias curriculum: Tools for empowering young children*. Washington, DC: National Association for the Education of Young Children.

Derman-Sparks, L., & Phillips, C. B. (1997). *Teaching/learning anti-racism: A developmental approach*. New York: Teachers College Press.

Doyle, A., & Aboud, F. E. (1993). Social and cognitive determinants of prejudice in children. In K. A. McLeod (Ed.), *Multicultural education: The state of the art* (pp. 28–33). Toronto: University of Toronto Press.

Feagin, J. (2000). *Racist America: Roots, current realities, and future reparations*. New York: Routledge.

Feagin, J., & Herman, V. (1995). *White racism: The basics*. New York: Routledge.

Foley, N. (2002). Becoming Hispanic: Mexican Americans and whiteness. In P. S. Rothenberg (Ed.), *White privilege: Essential readings on the other side of racism* (pp. 49–59). New York: Worth Publishers.

Fox, D. J., & Jordan, V. B. (1973). Racial preference and identification of black, American Chinese, and white children. *Genetic Psychology Monographs, 88*, 229–286.

Furby, L. (1979). Inequalities in personal possessions: Explanations for and judgments about unequal distribution. *Human Development, 22*, 180–202.

Furnham, A., & Stacey, B. (1991). *Young people's understanding of society*. New York: Routledge.

Glover, A. (1996). Children and bias. In B. Creaser & E. Dau (Eds.), *The anti-bias approach in early childhood* (pp. 1–16). Sydney, Australia: Harper Educational.

Goodman, M. (1952). *Race awareness in young children*. Cambridge, MA: Addison-Wesley.

Gossett, T. F. (1963). *Race: The history of an idea in America*. New York: Schocken Books.

Hallinan, M. T., & Teixeira, R. A. (1987). Opportunities and constraints: Black–white differences in the formation of interracial friendships. *Child Development, 58*, 1358–1371.

Heinz, J., Folbre, N., & The Center for Popular Economics. (2000). *The ultimate field guide to the U.S. economy.* New York: New Press.

Helms, J. E. (Ed.) (1990). *Black and white racial identity: Theory, research, and practice.* Westport, CT: Greenwood Press.

Helms, J. E. (1995). An update of Helms' white and people of color racial identity models. In J. Ponterotto, J. Casas, C. Suzuki, & C. Alexander (Eds.), *Handbook of multicultural counseling.* Thousand Oaks, CA: Sage.

Hill, L. D. (2001). *Connecting kids: Exploring diversity together.* Gabriola Island, British Columbia, Cananda: New Society.

Hirschfield, L. A. (1995). Do children have a theory of race? *Cognition, 54,* 209–252.

Hoffman, E. (1999a). *No fair to tigers/No es justo para los tigres.* St. Paul, MN: Redleaf Press.

Hoffman, E. (1999b). *Play lady/La señora juguetona.* St. Paul, MN: Redleaf Press.

Hoffman, E. (2000). *Heroines and heroes/Heroínas y heroes.* St. Paul, MN: Redleaf Press.

Hoffman, E. (2004). *Magic capes, amazing powers: Transforming superhero play in the classroom.* St. Paul, MN: Redleaf Press.

Hoffman, M. (2000). Empathy and moral development: Implications for caring and justice. Cambridge, UK: Cambridge University Press.

Holmes, R. (1995). *How young children perceive race.* New York: Sage.

Horton, M., with Kohl, J., & Kohl, H. (1998). *The long haul: An autobiography.* New York: Teachers College Press.

Howard, G. R. (1999). *We can't teach what we don't know.* New York: Teachers College Press.

Ignatiev, N. (1995). *How the Irish became white.* New York: Routledge.

Jacobson, T. (2003). *Confronting our discomforts: Clearing the way for anti-bias in early childhood.* Portsmouth, NH: Heinemann.

Johnson, D. W., & Johnson, R. T. (2000). The three Cs of reducing prejudice and discrimination. In S. Okamp (Ed.), *Reducing prejudice and discrimination* (pp. 239–268). Mahwah, NJ: Lawrence Erlbaum Associates.

Katz, L. G., & McClellan, D. E. (1998). *Fostering children's social competence: The teacher's role.* Washington, DC: National Association for the Education of Young Children.

Katz, P. A. (1976). The acquisition of racial attitudes in children. In P. A. Katz (Ed.), *Towards the elimination of racism* (pp. 125–154). New York: Pergamon.

Katz, P. A. (2003). Racists or tolerant multiculturalists? How do they begin? *American Psychologist, 58*(11), 897–909.

Katz, P. A., & Kofkin, J. A. (1997). Race, gender, and young children. In S. Luthar, J. Burack, D. Cicchetti, & J. Weisz (Eds.), *Developmental perspectives on risk and pathology* (pp. 51–74). New York: Cambridge University Press.

Kemple, K. M. (2004). *Let's be friends: Peer competence and social inclusion in early childhood programs.* New York: Teachers College Press.

Kendall, F. (1996). *Diversity in the classroom: New approaches to the education of young children* (2nd ed.). New York: Teachers College Press.

Kinchloe, J. L., Steinberg, S. R., Rodriguez, N. M., & Chennault, R. E. (1998). *White reign: Deploying whiteness in America.* New York: St. Martin's Griffin.

Kirchner, G. (2000). *Children's games from around the world* (2nd ed.). Boston: Allyn & Bacon.

Kissinger, K. (1994). *All the colors we are: The story of how we get our skin color.* St. Paul, MN: Redleaf Press.

Kivel, P. (2002). *Uprooting racism: How white people can work for racial justice* (Rev. ed.). Gabriola Island, Canada: New Society.

Kivel, P. (2004). *You call this a democracy? Who benefits, who pays and who really decides.* New York: Apex Press.

Kline, S. (1993). *Out of the garden: Toys and children's culture in the age of TV marketing.* London: Verso.

Knowles, L., & Prewitt, K. (Eds.). (1969). *Institutional racism in America.* Englewood Cliffs, NJ: Prentice Hall.

Kozol, J. (1991). *Savage inequalities.* New York: Crown.

Kutner, B. (1985). Patterns of mental functioning associated with prejudice in children. *Psychological Monographs, 72*(406), 1–48.

Leahy, R. (1983). The development of the conception of social class. In R. Leahy (Ed.), *The child's construction of inequality* (pp. 79–107). New York: Academic Press.

Leahy, R. (1990). The development of concepts of economic and social inequality. *New Directions for Child Development, 46,* 107–120.

Lee, R. (2004). *Developing measures to learn how multicultural activities affect children's attitudes about race and social class.* Senior Honors Thesis, Mount Holyoke College.

Lewis, A. E. (2001). There is no race in the school yard: Color-blind ideology in an all-white school. *American Educational Research Journal, 38*(4), 781–811.

Lipsitz, G. (2002). The possessive investment in whiteness. In P. S. Rothenberg (Ed.), *White privilege: Essential readings on the other side of racism* (pp. 61–85). New York: Worth.

Lowen, J. (1995). *Lies my teacher told me.* New York: Simon & Schuster.

Lowen, J. (1999). *Lies across America: What our historical sites get wrong.* New York: Simon & Schuster.

MacNaughton, G. (2004). Learning from young children about social diversity: Challenges for our equity practices in the classroom. In A. Van Keulen (Ed.), *Young children aren't biased, are they?!* (pp. 65–75). Amsterdam: SWP.

Maher, F., & Tetrault, M. K. T. (1998). "They got the paradigm and painted it white": Whiteness and pedagogies of positionality. In J. L. Kincheloe, S. R. Steinberg, N. M. Rodriguez, & R. E. Chennault (Eds.), *White reign: Deploying whiteness in America* (pp. 137–158). New York: St. Martin's Griffin.

Martin, B. Jr., (1970). *I am freedom's child.* New York: Bowmar.

McIntosh, P. (1995). White privilege and male privilege: A personal account of coming to see correspondences through work in women's studies. In M. L. Anderson & P. H. Collins (Eds.), *Race, class, and gender: An anthology* (pp. 76–87). Belmont, CA: Wadsworth.

McIntyre, A. (1997). *Making meaning of Whiteness: Exploring racial identity with white teachers.* Albany: State University of New York Press.

McLoyd, V. C., & Ceballo, R. (1998). Conceptualizing and assessing the economic context: Issues in the study of race and child development. In V. C.

McLoyd & L. Steinberg (Eds.), *Studying minority adolescents: Conceptual, methodological, and theoretical issues* (pp. 251–278). Mahwah, NJ: Lawrence Erlbaum.

Memmi, A. (1965). *The colonizer and the colonized*. Boston: Beacon Press.

Morland, J. K. (1962). Racial acceptance and preference of nursery school children in a southern city. *Merrill-Palmer Quarterly, 8*, 271–280.

Newman, M. A., Liss, M. B., & Sherman, F. (1983). Ethnic awareness in children: Not a unitary concept. *Journal of Genetic Psychology, 143*, 103–112.

O'Brien, E. (2001). *Whites confront racism: Antiracists and their paths to action.* Lanham, MD: Rowman & Littlefield.

Omi, M., & Winant, H. (1986). *Racial formation in the United States*. New York: Routledge & Kegan Paul.

Orlick, T. (1978). *The cooperative sports and games book: Challenge without competition.* New York: Pantheon.

Orlick, T. (1982). *The second cooperative sports and games book: Over 200 brand-new cooperative games for kids and adults and both.* Ann Arbor, MI: North American Students of Cooperation.

Pelo, A., & Davidson, F. (2000). *That's not fair: A teacher's guide to activism with young children.* St. Paul, MN: Redleaf Press.

Porter, J. D. (1971). *Black child, white child: The development of racial attitudes.* Cambridge, MA: Harvard University Press.

Radke, M., & Trager, H. G. (1950). Children's perceptions of the social roles of Negroes and whites. *Journal of Psychology, 29*, 3–33.

Ramsey, P. G. (1982, August). *Racial differences in children's contacts and comments about others.* Paper presented at the annual meeting of the American Psychological Association, Washington, DC.

Ramsey, P. G. (1983). *Young children's responses to racial differences: Socio-cultural perspectives.* Paper presented at the biennial meeting of the Society for Research in Child Development, Detroit.

Ramsey, P. G. (1987). Young children's thinking about ethnic differences. In J. Phinney & M. Rotheram (Eds.), *Children's ethnic socialization: Pluralism and development* (pp. 56–72). Beverly Hills, CA: Sage.

Ramsey, P. G. (1991a). *Making friends in school: Promoting peer relationships in early childhood.* New York: Teachers College Press.

Ramsey, P. G. (1991b). The salience of race in young children growing up in an all-white community. *Journal of Educational Psychology, 83*, 28–34.

Ramsey, P. G. (1991c). Young children's awareness and understanding of social class differences. *Journal of Genetic Psychology, 152*, 71–82.

Ramsey, P. G. (2004). *Teaching and learning in a diverse world* (3rd ed.). New York: Teachers College Press.

Ramsey, P. G., & Myers, L. C. (1990). Salience of race in young children's cognitive, affective and behavioral responses to social environments. *Journal of Applied Developmental Psychology, 11*, 49–67.

Ramsey, P. G., & Williams, L. R., with Vold, E. B. (2003). *Multicultural education: A source book* (2nd ed.). New York: RoutledgeFalmer.

Roediger, D. (1991). *The wages of whiteness: Race and the making of the American working class*. London: Verso.

Roediger, D. (2005). *Working toward whiteness: How America's immigrants became white*. New York: Basic Books.

Rogovin, P. (1998). *Classroom interviews: A world of learning*. Portsmouth, NH: Heinemann.

Rosenfield, D., & Stephan, W. G. (1981). Intergroup relations among children. In S. S. Brehm, S. M. Kassin, & F. X. Gibbons (Eds.), *Developmental social psychology* (pp. 271–297). New York: Oxford University Press.

Rothenberg, P. S. (2002). *White privilege: Essential readings on the other side of racism*. New York: Worth.

Ryan, W. (1976). *Blaming the victim* (Rev. ed.). New York: Vintage Books.

Silin, J. G. (1995). *Sex, death, and the education of children: Our passion for ignorance in the age of AIDS*. New York: Teachers College Press.

Singleton, L. C., & Asher, S. R. (1977). Peer preferences and social interaction among third-grade children in an integrated school district. *Journal of Educational Psychology, 69*, 330–336.

Slavin, R. E. (1995). Cooperative learning and intergroup relations. In J. A. Banks & C. A. M. Banks (Eds.), *Handbook of research on multicultural education* (pp. 628–634). New York: Macmillan.

Sleeter, C. E. (1994). White racism. *Multicultural Education, 1*, 5–8, 39.

Sleeter, C. E. (2001). *Culture, difference, and power* [CD ROM]. New York: Teachers College Press.

Smith, B. (1983). Homophobia: Why bring it up? *Interracial Books for Children Bulletin, 14*, 112–113.

Smith, L. (1962). *Killers of the dream* (Rev. ed.). New York: Norton. (Original work published 1949)

Stabler, J. R., Zeig, J. A., & Johnson, E. E. (1982). Perceptions of racially related stimuli by young children. *Perceptual and Motor Skills, 54*(1), 71–77.

Stalvey, L. M. (1989). *The education of a WASP*. Madison: University of Wisconsin Press.

Strope, L. (2004, August 17). Income gap in U.S. continues to widen. *The San Diego Union*, p. A7.

Takaki, R. (1993). *A different mirror: A history of multicultural America*. Boston: Little, Brown.

Tatum, B. D. (1992). Talking about race, learning about racism: The application of racial identity development theory in the classroom. *Harvard Educational Review, 62*(1), 1–24.

Tatum, B. D. (1994). Teaching white students about racism: The search for white allies and the restoration of hope. *Teachers College Record, 95*, 462–476.

Tatum, B. D. (1997). *"Why are all the black kids sitting together in the cafeteria?" and other conversations about race*. New York: Basic Books.

Terry, R. (1970). *For whites only*. Grand Rapids, MI: Eerdmans.

Thomas, M. (2005). On growing up white: Teachers relate their experiences. Unpublished manuscript.

Thomas, R. W. (1996). *Understanding interracial unity*. Thousand Oaks, CA: Sage.

Thurman, S. K., & Lewis, M. (1979). Children's responses to differences: Some possible implications for mainstreaming. *Exceptional Children, 45,* 468–470.

Trager, H., & Radke Yarrow, M. (1952). *They learn what they live: Prejudice in young children*. New York: Harper & Brothers.

Ulichny, P. (1994, April). *Cultures in conflict*. Paper presented at the annual meeting of the American Educational Research Association, New Orleans.

Van Ausdale, D., & Feagin, J. R. (2001). *The first R: How children learn race and racism*. Lanham, MD: Rowan & Littlefield.

Van Keulen, A. (2004). *Young children aren't biased, are they?!* Amsterdam: SWP.

Vorrasi, J. A., & Gabarino, J. (2000). Poverty and youth violence: Not all risk factors are created equal. In V. Polakow (Ed.), *The public assault on America's children: Poverty, violence, and juvenile injustice* (pp. 59–77). New York: Teachers College Press.

Vygotsky, L. S. (1978). *Mind in society: The development of higher psychological processes*. Cambridge, MA: Harvard University Press.

Weis, L., Proweller, A., & Centrie, C. (1997). Re-examining "A moment of history": Loss of privilege inside white working-class masculinity in the 1990s. In M. Fine, L. Weis, L. C. Powell, & L. M. Wong (Eds.), *Off white: Readings on race, power, and society* (pp. 210–226). New York: Routledge.

Wellman, D. (1977). *Portraits of white racism*. Cambridge, UK: Cambridge University Press.

Whitney, T. (1999). *Kids like us: Using persona dolls in the classroom*. St. Paul, MN: Redleaf Press.

Williams, J. E., & Morland, J. K. (1976). *Race, color, and the young child*. Chapel Hill: University of North Carolina Press.

Wise, T. (2005). *White like me: Reflections on race from a privileged son*. New York: Soft Skull Press.

Wolpert, E. (1999). *Start seeing diversity: The basic guide to an anti-bias classroom* [Video and Guide]. St. Paul, MN: Redleaf Press.

Wolpert, E. (2002). Redefining the norm: Early childhood anti-bias strategies. In E. Lee, D. Menkart, & M. Okazawa-Rey (Eds.), *Beyond heroes and holidays: A practical guide to K–12 anti-racist, multicultural education and staff development*. Washington, DC: Teaching for Change.

York, S. (2003). *Roots and wings: Affirming culture in early childhood programs* (Rev. ed.). St. Paul, MN: Redleaf Press.

Zinn, H. (1995). *A people's history of the United States: 1492–present*. (Rev. ed.). New York: HarperPerennial.

Zinn, H. (Ed.). (2004). *The people speak: American voices, some famous, some little known*. New York: Perennial Books.

Index

About the Authors

Louise Derman-Sparks is a longtime faculty member at Pacific Oaks College in Pasadena, California currently teaching online classes. She conducts workshops and consults throughout the United States and internationally and was on the Governing Board of the National Association for the Education of Young Children (1998–2001). Formerly, she taught in the Perry Preschool and the Ypsilanti Early Childhood Projects, and was a child-care center director. She holds a master's degree in Education from the University of Michigan.

Patricia G. Ramsey is Professor of Psychology and Education and Director of Gorse Child Study Center at Mount Holyoke College in South Hadley, Massachusetts. Formerly, she taught in the Early Childhood Education Departments at Wheelock College, Indiana University, and the University of Massachusetts. She holds a master's degree from California State University in San Francisco and a doctorate in early childhood education from the University of Massachusetts in Amherst. She is a former preschool and kindergarten teacher.